After Winter Comes Spring

A Journey Through Grief and Beyond

Ann G. Boulet

After Winter Comes Spring: A Journey Through Grief and Beyond
Copyright © 2022 Ann G. Boulet

Produced and printed by Stillwater River Publications. All rights reserved. Written and produced in the United States of America. This book may not be reproduced or sold in any form without the expressed, written permission of the author and publisher.

Visit our website at **www.StillwaterPress.com** for more information.

First Stillwater River Publications Edition.

ISBN: 978-1-958217-71-9

Library of Congress Control Number: 2022920746

1 2 3 4 5 6 7 8 9 10
Written by Ann G. Boulet.
Cover & interior book design by Matthew St. Jean.
Published by Stillwater River Publications, Pawtucket, RI, USA.

Names: Boulet, Ann G., author.
Title: After winter comes spring : a journey through grief
and beyond / Ann G. Boulet.
Description: First Stillwater River Publications edition. | Pawtucket, RI, USA : Stillwater River Publications, [2022]
Identifiers: ISBN: 978-1-958217-71-9 | LCCN: 2022920746
Subjects: LCSH: Boulet, Ann G. | Grief. | Widows--Biography. | Loss (Psychology) | Death-- Psychological aspects. | Mental healing. | LCGFT: Self-help publications.

Some names have been changed to protect the privacy of those involved.

The views and opinions expressed in this book are solely those of the author and do not necessarily reflect the views and opinions of the publisher.

*To my son and daughter,
you gave me a purpose for moving ahead
after your dad died! Without the two of you
I'm not sure I could have survived this journey!*

*To my granddaughter and grandsons,
you always put a smile on Nona's face.
And I'm sure Poppy is smiling too!*

*To Big Guy,
you brought spring into my life!
And you have continually encouraged me
to share my journey with others.*

Contents

Preface .... *vii*
Introduction .... *x*

Manner of Death 1
The Aftermath 6
"Happy" New Year 11
Preparations 14
In the Meantime 18
Rituals 23
Subsequent Days 32
The Actual Beginnings of Widowhood 36
Physicians and Therapists 41
Busyness 48
A Cry for Help 51
Road to Recovery 56
My "Blue" Room 65
Tears 69
Secondary Losses 74
Feeling His Presence 76
Pennies from Heaven 80
Going It Alone 83
Mission in Life 86

Throughout the Years 93
Spring Came Along Totally Unexpected 97
And the Grief Goes On 102
What About God? 105
Afterword 110

Works Cited *112*
Acknowledgments *118*
About the Author *120*

Preface

THIS BOOK WAS ORIGINALLY WRITTEN AS A SCHOLarly project and final requirement for a Certificate in Thanatology from Mount Ida College in Dedham, Massachusetts. I began it in 2007, worked on it in various time intervals, and completed it in 2008. My main purpose was to describe my own journey through grief after the death of my husband. However, because it was fulfilling an academic requirement, it could not be solely a personal journal. Therefore, documentation from various authors and authorities in the field of thanatology was provided within the context of my personal experiences. In so doing I displayed the knowledge gained through workshops and courses taken at the University of Rhode Island and Mount Ida College as well as through personal reading.

With the certificate from the college and certification I obtained from the Association for Death Education and Counseling, I had plans for a second career in bereavement when I retired from the field of education in 2010. At that time I had hoped to work with a funeral home on "aftercare" of families. I have always believed that not enough attention is given to those left behind, especially when a death is sudden and unexpected and not a result of illness. I also think that society keeps people from grieving and eventually moving on because of the "get over it" attitude still prevalent today. However, my goal and my enthusiasm were squelched by the economy.

Consequently, my bereavement work was reduced to informal outreach to people who had experienced a loss. I also gave occasional talks on grief and loss to individuals of all ages, from high school students to seniors. But I have always wanted to reach more individuals because I believe I have something to offer others who are experiencing grief. It's not just my studies; it's my personal experience of loss of a loved one.

When I wrote my original project, I found it to be cathartic for me. But in the back of my mind I had hoped it would serve as a resource for other widows on their own journey of grief.

More than several individuals, not all widows, read my original manuscript and found it helpful. These same people encouraged me to reach others through publishing it. As a result, I decided to expand my work, and bring events and details up to date. And because of its original style I continued to include references to other works/authors. However, I had hoped the resulting book would not be looked upon as an academic project. Rather, I wanted it to provide some good information while opening the door for readers to investigate authorities in the field of death and dying, other writers who share their own journeys, and novelists who bring the topic of death into their works through the lives of their characters.

For one reason or another even the expanded "version" of my manuscript never saw publication. To further delay it, someone came into my life, plus I downsized and moved from a house to a condo; and consequently, my book has been on the back burner for over a decade. I should have worked on it during the Covid months of 2020 but I didn't. Then I thought 2021 would be the year to see myself reach my goal of publication but an unexpected health event deferred it longer. Hopefully, 2022 will be the year of fruition, especially since Al and I would have celebrated our fiftieth wedding anniversary this year!

Introduction

In September of 1994 my husband Al lost his job as the controller of a manufacturing company. Although both of us were very upset by this, we didn't panic. I was teaching, and consequently we had health coverage. Our son was in his junior year of college and our daughter was in her third year of high school. We told our children that their job was to do their very best in school and leave the rest to us.

Although my husband had been given a three months' severance package, he became resolved to the fact that finding a new position would take him six to nine months. During that time he seemed okay but once that period passed, his spirits began to wane. I really worried about him. He seemed so discouraged even though he was able to do some consulting work. Somehow we managed.

Finally, after eighteen months of unemployment he was able to secure a job as the controller of another manufacturing company. Although it was in another state, Al was resigned to the ninety-mile round trip commute. For him the distance seemed like a small price to pay to feel productive again. Thus, his period of unemployment officially ended on March 27, 1996.

Al's birthday was April 8. After all he had endured, I wanted to give him something meaningful and special. One of my colleagues suggested a book entitled *The Tree That Survived the Winter* by Mary Fahy. She said it was a book about survival and the title alone made it seem so appropriate as a gift. Within this book I wrote:

Al,

The winter was long but you survived—September 13, 1994 to March 27, 1996—thanks to your faith and those who love you. If another winter should come your way, know that you are a survivor!

Love always,

Ann

4-8-96

Al seemed to like the book but I never knew what he did with it. Shortly after his death, my son decided to go up to his father's office since he had never had a chance to see it. Upon his return, he informed me that my husband's boss had given him a box of Al's belongings. Initially I had forgotten about the box, but later that evening I saw it downstairs in the study. As I went through the contents, I found old accounting books that had been Al's in college, some pictures of the family including pictures of his parents and of him as a child, his mug collection and Fahy's book. At that moment I felt Al's presence; it was as if he were giving the book back to me and telling me that everything would be all right, that I would survive his death and life without him. As the authors of the book *Hello from Heaven* have stated, "It appears that our deceased loved ones can still be there for us even when we need them the most. They can often be a source of comfort and strength to draw upon during our most difficult life situations" (Guggenheim and Guggenheim 31). From that point forward I knew that I would be okay. Hence, my idea of equating grief with winter had its beginnings.

Ironically, the autumn before Al's death, we had to make a decision about transplanting an Alberta spruce on the side of our house. The spring before, a landscaper who later proved to be incompetent took three of them from another part of the yard and placed them on the side near our bedroom. Unfortunately two of the three did not survive. When Al tried to remove them, they came out effortlessly proving to us that they had not been replanted properly. The third positioned at one end was out of place by itself and looked like the Lone Ranger. When we checked into replacing the other two, the price of full-grown shrubs made that project not an option. And when we consulted with another landscaper, we were told that transplanting the last one to the center would not be feasible and would lead to its death as well.

However, I felt it was worth trying on our own. Al did have trouble getting that last healthy shrub out of the ground. It seemed like it didn't want to budge. As he was struggling with it, I could see him questioning my insistence that it be right in the middle. Actually, moving it brought it much closer to our bedroom window and it could be viewed from there. Little did I know that shrub would come to be my symbol of survival. Somehow, some way, that shrub survived that first winter in its new position, the winter when Al died. And as the years passed that shrub seemed healthier and greener than ever before. So it was that I often found myself glancing out of the bedroom window whenever I needed a reminder that like that Alberta spruce I would survive the winter. However, my winter would not be merely one season of three months. Back then I felt it would be the rest of my life. Hence, the reason the original title of my manuscript was *Neverending Winter: A Journey of Grief.*

But looking at winter as a season with cold dreary days as well as days of sun and warmth made the whole process more manageable. Robert Neimeyer explains the use of metaphoric images as a means of coping with loss:

> Sometimes literal words fail us in conveying our unique sense of loss—we may feel depressed, desolate, alone, or angry, but the character of our own grief is somehow more than just the sum of these standard descriptions. To move beyond the constraints of public speech, we need to use words in a more personal way, and draw on terms that are rich in resonance and imagery. Speaking of our loss metaphorically can help us accomplish this, sometimes leading to surprising insights unavailable to us when we think of it only in more conventional, "symptomatic terms." (172)

After Winter Comes Spring

Manner of Death

"EVERY LIFE IS DIFFERENT FROM ANY OTHER THAT has gone before it, and so is every death. The uniqueness of us extends even to the way we die" (Nuland 3).

On December 31, 1999 Y2K was on everyone's mind. This applied especially to my husband Al since he was the controller of a company and the threat of computer turmoil concerned him. However, Y2K became the least of our problems since my husband died that afternoon while sitting in his favorite recliner.

Approximately thirty minutes before, he had complained about not feeling well. When he told me his jaw and arm hurt, I remember asking him if he thought he might be having a heart attack. My daughter Jenny, who with her friend Kathleen was getting ready for an evening out, gave me a look of annoyance since I had always been a hypochondriac. My husband neither denied nor confirmed the suggestion. I did look in the closet for some aspirin but remembered that I had recently thrown out some that were past expiration. Of course, neither of us thought about the low dose ones that were part of Al's daily routine. Ironically, I even remember looking up "heart attack" in the medical dictionary; but since I always tend to overreact when illness is concerned, I did not consider that action one of panic or concern. How I wish I had! "Another strong preoccupation is with feelings of guilt. The bereaved searches the time before the death for evidence of failure to do right by the lost one. He accuses himself of negligence and exaggerates minor omissions" (Lindemann 187).

I suggested that we go down to the family room and relax while watching a movie together. Al and I were supposed to go out for supper later with some friends and were then going back to their house to toast in the New Year. We had even chilled a bottle of champagne that friends from France had given us for Christmas. So as Al settled into his favorite recliner, I assured him that we could just stay home that evening if he still didn't feel better. He nodded in agreement.

Earlier that day I had rented a couple of movies for us to watch. After I put one of the movies in the VCR, I handed Al the remote and told him to pause it if it progressed to the feature before I returned. I went upstairs with some folded laundry. I know I wasn't gone more than a few minutes. When I returned, Al handed me the remote and said the upcoming attractions were still being shown. I couldn't have been sitting more than a minute when I heard a loud gasping type of sound. I looked at Al and saw that his head was slumped to the side. I screamed for Jenny and immediately called 911. She came down and the two of us tried to get him to breathe. Although both of us had had CPR training at some point in the past, neither of us could think to perform it correctly. In spite of that, we did make some effort to get him to breathe. It seemed like an eternity and still no one came in response to my 911 call. So I called again.

My daughter and I were beside ourselves. Although it seemed like forever before the rescue crew arrived, I later learned that in reality the response time had been reasonable. I remember Jenny being out in the driveway waiting for the truck and flagging it down once it came into sight. The team came in and placed Al on the floor and began to work on him. Again the time seemed never-ending but again in reality was not that long.

The EMTs said they were going to take my husband to the hospital. I asked if he was going to be all right and I don't remember their answering me one way or another. I remember thinking that Al was dead, right there in his own home. I said that I wanted to ride along. They told me I had to go up front. I think that should have been my clue that things were not good. Again it seemed like such a long time before the rescue finally left for the hospital. Jenny followed in one of our cars driven by Kathleen.

The ride to the hospital seemed like it took forever. I can't remember if they used the siren; something makes me think they didn't—that it wasn't necessary. Upon arrival at the hospital I was directed to the emergency room admission desk.

After waiting there just a minute and feeling frustrated, I pushed my way into another area. Then I was led into a small room where a woman came to take information. I could barely think to answer her questions. There I was being asked information about home, phone, etc., while my husband lay dying or dead in another room.

As soon as I saw the doctor and a priest come into the room, I knew the inevitable. But I still asked the question. "Is my husband dead?" The doctor just stood there saying nothing. He didn't have to; I knew.

I'm still surprised that I remained calm. I asked to see Al; I wanted to be with my husband. A nurse brought me in and left me alone with him. It all seemed unreal—his lying there covered with a sheet up to his neck and with a tube in his mouth. I just sat there looking at him. I'm not sure how long I stayed with him. It seemed like a lifetime but again time seems endless when there's a tragedy. I remember kissing Al's forehead and not being sure what I was "allowed" to do. When I read what Dr. Joyce Brothers did when she was with her husband after he had died, I became saddened and jealous. "They left me alone with him. I kissed him. I kissed his hands and I kissed his eyes and I kissed his head and I cried" (67). Why I didn't do more still remains a mystery to me!

I sometimes wonder why we went to the hospital. Why the big show of bringing Al there to make it appear that there was a chance of saving him when in reality I knew he was dead before we even left the house. Why didn't they just pronounce him dead in his own surroundings rather than in the cold, austere environment of that trauma room? And why didn't they let me be there with him when they knew there was no longer any life in him? I hear it's called standard hospital procedure. I guess my one consolation is that I was with Al when he died in his own home in his favorite recliner.

> Nowadays, very few of us actually witness the deaths of those we love. Not many people die at home anymore, and those who do are usually victims of drawn-out diseases or chronic degenerative conditions in which drugging and narcosis effectively hide the biological events that are occurring. Of the approximately 80 percent of Americans who die in a hospital, almost all are in large part concealed, or at least the details of the final approach to mortality are concealed, from those who have been closest to them in life. (Nuland 8)

The Aftermath

On December 30, 2003 author Joan Didion sat across from her husband John Gregory Dunne as he suffered a massive fatal attack. In her book entitled *The Year of Magical Thinking* she repeatedly wrote:

> Life changes fast.
> Life changes in an instant.
> You sit down to dinner and life as you know it ends.
> (3)

Those could have been my words, only the last line would be changed to: "You sit down to watch a movie and life as you know it ends."

I remember coming out of the room and leaving my husband behind. I saw my daughter scrunched against a wall crying. Her friend was timidly waiting in a side room. She was so sensitive not to intrude on this very private time in our lives.

I can't remember much about the ride home. Did we make small talk? Did we talk about what should be done once we got home? What phone calls we should make?

"...death comes as a terrifying shock, leaving the bereaved unprepared and adrift" (Diamant 4).

When we did get home, I remember there being a message from my son James who was living in Atlanta at the time. He sounded upset and asked that I call him. Strangely, I assumed someone had called him with the news of his father's death. I was wrong. He was calling about a problem he was having with one of his professors. Not knowing this, however, I began by saying that there was nothing that could have been done. He asked what I was talking about. I had to tell him his father had had a heart attack. He said he would leave immediately. I then had to tell him it was too late, that his dad was already dead.

The next hour or two involved trying to get my son a flight home. He was determined to drive. After much convincing at both ends, we here and his friends down there, a flight was arranged for seven o'clock that evening. A friend would take him to the airport and a relative would pick him up.

Amidst all this we also received what I considered a very ill-timed call. My daughter had answered it. It was someone from the hospital calling to see if we wanted to donate my husband's organs. I later learned the doctor should have mentioned something about that when we were still at the hospital. "There is a question of when organ donation should be mentioned as a possibility....Those who see saving lives through transplantation as their main obligation will have little trouble justifying the mention of organ donation if it will yield an organ that would otherwise not have been available for transplantation" (Zucker 110). I thought about how much my husband hated doctors and hospitals and anything connected to them.

And ironically, the topic had come up several months before. Al noticed that I had signed an organ donation card. When he saw it, he made a face and seemed to shudder. In his own way Al had made his wishes known to me beforehand. So I knew that I had to say "absolutely not" to the hospital's request.

Then I had to make a call to the funeral home. The funeral director was a man whom my husband's family had known well. When I told him that Al had died, he remained very businesslike in his tone. That was something that surprised me but deep down I knew that was his role, to be the stabilizer in such a situation. I told him that the hospital had informed me that, since my husband had died suddenly, the medical examiner might require that an autopsy be performed.

Again, knowing how my husband couldn't even stand to have blood work done, I cringed at the thought of his body being mutilated. In the end the medical examiner was satisfied that the cause of my husband's death was myocardial infarction and did not order the autopsy.

In hindsight, I wish he had. Or maybe I should have requested one. I think now about my children and wonder if more information about their father's death would be helpful for their own health. "With genetics being found to play a bigger role in a wider range of conditions, some medical experts believe that accurately knowing a family member's cause of death provides valuable information that can potentially save lives" (DeSpelder and Strictland 180).

After those calls were made, the task of notifying relatives and friends lay on my daughter. I had always considered her to be more vulnerable than my son, probably because she had always been shy growing up. How wrong I was! I think back and feel so bad that I placed that burden on her shoulders. Jenny was such a trooper making those dreaded calls. And her friend Kathleen was such a sweetheart. She made tea for us and tried to stay available to help, but always in the background.

Before long, friends and relatives began arriving at the house. I really don't remember much about that; just that I couldn't wait for my son to get home. I remember my eighty-one-year-old mother calling me and saying how sorry she was. I had now joined her on the road of widowhood. She wanted to come to be with me but I thought it best that she remain home. I could tell by her voice how shaken she was by this whole event. Al's parents had both died in 1989 and technically my mother had been the only surrogate "parental" figure in his life since then.

I couldn't even think about food but fortunately others did. I saw food being served to the guests who might be hungry. I later learned that the parents of my daughter's heart sister Alyssa had gone out and bought pizza. It's amazing! All my life I had been an emotional eater. And now, though filled with emotions of sadness and disbelief, I couldn't stand the thought of food. It was as if my throat had closed up.

Once James arrived home, I felt a sense of relief. He came in and immediately hugged me. I don't remember if I cried. Wouldn't that be something I should remember? I don't recall when people left, and my children and I were alone. I do remember my son calling the hospital to ask about my husband's rosary beads which he always carried in his pocket. He was told that the funeral director had already picked up the body and his belongings since the medical examiner was satisfied with the attending physician's ruling.

But what about my heart? What finding could be made about it? It felt like it had a huge hole in it—such a void and not even twelve hours had passed! "If you gave someone your heart and they died, did they take it with them? Did you spend the rest of forever with a hole inside you that couldn't be filled?" (Picoult 102).

We decided we should get some sleep. Thinking back now, I don't remember having any sense of when midnight struck and the New Year began. Jenny asked if she could sleep in my bed with me. James went into his own room but it wasn't long before I could hear him walking around. I told him to join us on the bed. "How can we all fit?" he asked. I assured him we would; we needed to be together. And so we spent the night tossing and turning but holding on to each other for comfort and security at this, the worst possible time in our lives. "No one ever told me that grief felt so like fear. I am not afraid, but the sensation is like being afraid. That same fluttering in the stomach, the same restlessness, the yawning. I keep on swallowing" (Lewis 1).

"Happy" New Year

I DON'T THINK ANY OF US GOT ANY REAL SLEEP. I WAS up very early to call relatives in Italy and friends in France. Looking back I find it so odd that I would reach out to them. I think I felt the need to let the whole world know that my husband had died. Was this my way of facing reality—making something that seemed so unreal, real? I don't know!

The French say "Bonne Année" which literally means Good Year. I then told my friend that it wasn't a good year, that it was a sad year. Aside from her telling me how sorry she was, I really don't remember anything else about our conversation. My next call to relatives in Italy involved basically the same type of conversation.

Later I showered and dressed and positioned myself on the living room sofa. I remember wearing black slacks and a black sweater. How strange that I did this without even thinking! Black had always been a sign of mourning, but over the years, people have gotten away from it. Was this a carryover from when I was a child growing up? Whenever

I used to see people dressed in black, there was always a certain reverence towards them, a sense of gentleness because it was known that they were dealing with a loss in their lives. Is that what I was looking for? "Handle me gently. I have a hole in my heart!" A passage in a novel by Ann Hood validates what I continue to believe today. "Angelina always wore a black shawl over her head, and thick-soled black shoes, and a black dress. 'People should know you're in mourning,' she'd told Mary. 'When you wear black, they understand'" (Hood, *The Knitting Circle* 16).

I remember calling the funeral director and setting up an appointment for the next day. Because of the holidays there had been a backlog, so no need to rush in to see him that day. He told me that most likely the funeral wouldn't be until the following Wednesday, so it was going to be a long, drawn-out time for us.

More friends and relatives stopped by to express their condolences; more friends and relatives who lived out of state were notified. Aside from that I really don't remember much. Thinking back I know it was a Saturday, but it just didn't feel like it. And it definitely didn't feel like a holiday.

Years ago when my children were small we had begun a little New Year's tradition with Al's parents. My father-in-law was of French-Canadian descent and he always used to talk about his mother's meat pie that was served on New Year's Day. One year I decided to surprise him. I asked my mother-in-law for the ingredients and set about duplicating this dish. I can still remember how excited my father-in-law was when he took that first forkful of my creation. I think he paid me the highest compliment when he told me it tasted just like his mom's. Even after Al's parents died, we continued this tradition and would often invite friends or relatives to join us. More recently, Al had added to this simple meal. We had learned from friends that lentil soup was usually served on this day as a sign of good luck for the coming year.

And so it was that the lentil soup Al had made the day before, actually the last thing he had done in the kitchen, was offered along with meat pie to anyone who visited that day. I did put some soup in containers and froze it. I knew I would need a connection to my husband in the months to follow. While his soup was gone within the first half of the year, lentil soup remained a comfort food for me whenever I needed to feel connected to Al.

> We are often comforted by preserving in our lives objects that belonged to the persons we have lost, and quite naturally tend to accumulate keepsakes and mementos of people and times that have gone before. Occasionally it is helpful to adopt this as a conscious strategy for responding to loss, by making deliberate decisions about how to integrate cherished "linking objects" into our ongoing lives. (Neimeyer 152)

Preparations

It felt surreal going to the funeral home. Before we left the house, I had tried to compose an obituary that would be placed in the local paper. It was a task easier said than done.

When we arrived, Rudy was there waiting for us. He hugged me and offered his condolences to my children and me. He then introduced us to Tim, an associate, and told us Tim would be taking care of us. At the time I felt a little disappointed since Rudy had known my husband and his family for so many years, and now the making of my husband's arrangements had been given over to a "stranger." It was only later that I would learn that Rudy's involvement had been limited because of some health issues. And I would come to realize what a blessing Tim was in our lives!

As we were going downstairs, James excused himself and told us he would join us momentarily. Later I discovered that he had contacted Rudy and requested seeing his father's body. Since he hadn't been there when Al died, and the last time he had seen him was before he returned to Georgia after Christmas, I think he needed visual proof that his father had indeed died, and time alone with him. "Death is hardest to comprehend without any forewarning. The news and loss are crushing....in sudden death, the denial will be longer and deeper" (Kübler-Ross and Kessler 195).

The first half of the tasks at hand included calling hours, the service, the burial, announcements, etc. We seemed to get through those decisions without any major difficulties. Then it was time to choose a casket. Tim opened some doors nearby and led us into the "showroom." There we were faced with boxes that had a wide range of expense. I kept looking at them and then I began to cry. How could I be expected to make such a major decision! I had spent more than half my life with this man and now I had to make a choice that was technically being based on visual appeal and price. "Most people feel that the casket is the centerpiece of a funeral because of its symbolic and emotional value in honoring the deceased" (DeSpelder and Strictland 328).

Tim was so professional! He offered me a tissue and then said that he would leave us alone for a while but would be upstairs if we needed him. I don't think he wanted me to feel pressured by his presence. I kept looking around at the different styles and colors. Then I saw it! I know it seems strange but I wondered why I hadn't seen it before. It was a very simple but beautiful cherry wood casket. All I could think of was that it was very executive looking, perfect for the businessman that my husband had been. My children agreed that it was a good choice.

And so the arrangements were completed. Al's obituary would appear in the paper the next day as well as the day of the calling hours. His funeral would be held on Wednesday. And this was only Sunday! I would go to the cemetery the next day to choose a plot since there was no room at Al's family's plot. And I would also bring clothes to the funeral home.

We left there and headed home. Later a discussion arose regarding the coffin I had chosen. Was I sure I wanted to spend that amount of money on one? As I explained, I didn't feel like I had overspent or gone to extremes. I spent what I felt I needed to. My husband had always taken care of me throughout our marriage; I had to take care of him now in death. "Unlike the fast food restaurant, where value is determined solely by the cost, the value of death rituals should be determined by the comfort and consolation they provide to the bereaved" (Weeks 188).

I don't remember much about the rest of that day. Again, as people found out the news, calls and visits followed. One call and ensuing visit made a lasting impression on me. It was from a college student that Al had mentored at his local Alma Mater. As part of a new program at the university, freshmen were matched up with individuals who worked in their field of study. The mentorship was supposed to last a few months, time just enough to get the student acclimated to the new collegiate surroundings. But Al and Tony got along so well that it had extended into Tony's sophomore year. It was not unusual for him to come to supper occasionally at our house or for Al and him to meet for coffee and chat. I had called Tony and left a message for him at his apartment. He had been away for the holidays and had returned that evening. When he called, he sounded like he was in shock. On the phone Tony asked if he could visit. I told him he would always be welcome at the house. He said that he meant that evening; could he come up that evening? I can still remember Tony sitting in the dining area and looking towards the door. He said he kept expecting Al to walk in at any moment. I think this was something we were all hoping. "Why is it so hard for us to accept the finality of death? We do not willingly let go of a dearly loved person...." (Sanders 41).

In the Meantime

THE FOLLOWING DAY WAS TO BE JAM-PACKED. I had to go to my friend Lynne's art studio, the florist, the funeral home and the cemetery.

I had spent some time the night before sorting through photos for a collage to be displayed at the funeral home. "Photographs, perhaps more than any other form of memento, provide ways of memorializing the lives of those we have loved. At least as important as their private function in fostering our symbolic connection to a person who has died, is their public function in prompting shared reminiscence about that person" (Neimeyer 184).

There were so many photos that I became frustrated and ended up bringing a stack to Lynne and told her to use her judgment. Throughout the years I used to look at the beautiful collage so professionally done as it hung in my study and while Lynne's choices were good ones, I sometimes thought of other pictures I would have liked included. But at that time making a decision, even about pictures, was too difficult for me because grief had taken over my mind!

"Anytime someone you loved died, the world was suddenly smaller and less interesting and you, too, were diminished. They said that these events gave you perspective but that was sentimental. Perspective was what you had before the death, and after it you were so heavy-hearted and blurred of mind that you could not decide the simplest things...." (Just 17-18).

In order that flowers be kept to a minimum, we had requested that in lieu of flowers, donations to two charities be made in Al's memory. So I chose a simple arrangement from the children and me.

The night before I had carefully chosen the clothes that would be Al's last resting outfit. Ironically, I had put out his clothes for work each day for our entire married life. I chose his favorite blue suit and a tie he had bought himself when he was unemployed and first going on interviews. I also had a new shirt that I was waiting to return since I had bought the wrong neck size. Wrong neck size really wouldn't make a difference now. His socks were brand new. Jenny had purchased them for her father at the Guinness Brewery in Ireland when she had studied abroad in the fall. And then we had to have a pack of cigarettes placed in the inside of his sock. This dated back to Al's navy days when he had no pocket in his uniform shirt for them. In his pants pocket I wanted the pouch with his broken rosary beads which he still carried even after I had bought new ones for him. The new ones, of course, would be in his hands. I also wanted him laid out with his eyeglasses since he had always worn them. I was also very specific about his ring and his watch.

I wanted his good wedding band on for the calling hours but wanted him buried with his everyday band—the one he had gotten when we were first married. And then I wanted his dress watch on for the calling hours but the watch he wore every day to work put on later. Surprisingly, this latter request caused a little problem.

The day of the funeral Tim approached me and said that he had had trouble when he went to change watches. The one Al had always worn to work kept scratching his wrist no matter how Tim adjusted it. He asked me what I wanted to do. I told him to give me the watch; that for some reason Al didn't "want" that watch on.

It was about a year later that I realized the reason behind my husband's "message." A dear friend had asked me if he could have something of Al's as a remembrance. I carefully thought about what I could give Bob aside from something like a tie or T-shirt. It was then the watch came to mind. I had put aside Al's good one for James and really hadn't thought about what I would do with the other one. When I gave Bob the watch, he was thrilled. I told him it was Al's work watch and since he and Al were both hardworking family men, I thought it was appropriate that he should have it. And how ironic that Bob loved watches and collected them, something I hadn't known. Somehow his friend Al knew and made sure he conveyed his message to me. "Many people...reported experiencing an unusual physical occurrence following the death of a relative or friend. They regard these events as messages from their deceased loved ones. We call them ADCs of physical phenomena, which are a rather common type of after-death communication" (Guggenheim and Guggenheim 195).

While I was running all these errands, Jenny had gone to Boston. Since her classes were beginning that day, she wanted to meet with the dean and also let her professors know she would be out that week. James remained at home because he wasn't feeling well. I wasn't sure if it was nerves or the beginning of a bug.

At the cemetery the superintendent brought me out to show me which plots were available at that time. I remember it being an overcast day. I also remember one plot was facing east and the other west. I kept wondering which way I wanted to be facing each time I would visit in the future. It was difficult to imagine since the entire area seemed so barren; there were so few graves in this new section. I finally settled on one that would have the gravestone facing west, but I would be facing east when standing in front of it. There were trees in the background—I needed a surrounding that wouldn't be depressing if that were possible in such a setting. Once the paperwork for the plot was completed, I returned home to find James feeling better. This led me to believe that choosing a cemetery lot was something he just couldn't handle.

The next day brought a slow morning as we awaited the afternoon calling hours. Because Al had loved his home so much, the children had convinced me to have a catered collation after the funeral as opposed to a meal at a nearby restaurant.

> When we love family members, companions, or friends, we care about what they care about. What matters to them matters to us *because* we see how

much it matters to them....We come to share some of their interests, concerns, values, hopes, and dreams.

We can continue to care about what family members, companions, friends and public figures care about after they died. As we thrive in activities, experiences, and ways of being ourselves that derive from having known them and loved them, we continue loving them. (Attig 52-53)

Not knowing exactly how many people would be coming to the collation, I somehow knew it would be tight and was looking for ways to make more space for seating. A spur-of-the-moment decision led to my "taking down" the Christmas tree and placing it in the backyard in full view.

Neighbors had stepped in with offers to stay at the house that afternoon/evening. Another had offered to be there the next day and basically took over the hosting job that she knew I couldn't handle. I should add that never once did my children and I have to worry about food. There was an abundance of it from family, friends, and acquaintances. From this latter experience I learned and adopted that idea—food is what I can bring to the grieving. They have no sense of providing it for themselves but are so appreciative of it since keeping up one's strength is so important.

Rituals

"Rituals help us pass from one state of being to another....Funerary rites first separate the deceased from the land of the living and then help incorporate them into the world of the dead" (Zeitlin and Harlow 108).

IT WAS SUGGESTED THAT WE ARRIVE AT THE FUNERAL home a little earlier so that we could have time for ourselves. Rudy was there waiting for us. He led us into the room. I don't remember crying when I saw Al in the casket. I guess it's the numbness that overtakes a person. All I can remember is how natural and handsome he looked. Rudy asked me if I was happy with Al's appearance. I nodded in the affirmative. Al looked like he was sleeping. He looked so businesslike in his suit. His hair, his beard—nothing seemed amiss. "How could he not just be sleeping?" I thought to myself.

Some critics (such as Morgan & Morgan, 2001) have argued that many aspects of contemporary

> American funeral practices draw too much attention to the *body* itself. On this view, making real the implications of death is concerned primarily with taking leave of the *person* as part of an overall process of restructuring relationships with that person. Because a person is not only a body, or so this argument goes, it is the loss of the person, not his or her body, that is the primary concern. In this sense, the gathering of family and friends is a social validation of significant relationships and the reality of death. (Coor, Nabe, and Corr 281)

Before long, people began arriving to pay their respects. In the background we had requested that the music of Al's favorite singer be played. During the year prior to his death Al had fallen in love with the music of Andrea Bocelli. And so as people streamed through that afternoon/evening, the music Al so loved filled the room in a gentle tone.

I stood steadfastly during the entire wake. I think back and realize now that I felt I had to stay strong for my children. Although at times I cried, tears sparked by certain individuals, for the most part I held my composure.

After a very long five hours, the evening came to an end. We returned home with a few friends coming over for coffee, nothing like the usual group that used to be a typical Italian tradition after a wake.

The next day was cold but sunny. That was good. Since Al had always been the optimist in our family, maybe this was his way of saying that we should look on the bright side even in our sadness.

The children and I waited for the limousine to pick us up. Ironically, the gentleman driving was named Al. At the funeral home we did our hugging beforehand while no one was around. James and Jenny had papers they wanted added to their father's breast pocket. I didn't question them. This I know was part of their mourning.

We sat and others began arriving in preparation for the funeral. Tim came up to me and told me he had to stay behind but that another gentleman would accompany us and be in charge. He told me he would stop by the house later in the day with the floral arrangements. Because of our request for donations to charities, flowers were at a minimum. But I still couldn't see the flowers that were there all being brought to the cemetery to freeze. My daughter and I planned to bring them to some nursing homes in the area. That way they could be put to use in their chapels or as one home did—placed in individual vases for the people celebrating birthdays that month. We had only one spray placed at the grave.

One of the attendants began calling people to their cars and before long the room had emptied, leaving only the children and me and the pallbearers. We said our final goodbyes and proceeded to the limousine. Our driver came to the car and handed us the flag that had been placed inside the coffin during the wake. Although Al had served in the Navy, we decided against a military funeral that would have involved volleys being fired at the cemetery. Al and I unfortunately never really expressed our wishes regarding our funerals but there were things that had come up that made me sure I was doing what he would have chosen. He had never wanted shots at his father's funeral; he found them too upsetting I think.

It was about a half-hour ride to the church. Once there we waited in the car until everyone else had entered. When James was home on Monday, he had prepared a leaflet with the translated words of a song Al had wanted played at his funeral. Ironically he had made this intention known on more than one occasion. It wasn't a usual church song but we felt it needed to be played. It was a song by Andrea Bocelli entitled "Con Te Partirò—Time to Say Goodbye." As people entered the church, they were each given one of these papers.

I had also taken the time to select other music that I knew Al would have wanted. They included the following songs: "Be Not Afraid," "Shepherd Me, O God," "On Eagles' Wings," "I Have Loved You," and of course, a song played at our wedding, "Ave Maria." We had Bob play the guitar and Alyssa sing.

I also chose meaningful objects that would be brought up as part of the Offertory Procession: Al's briefcase to symbolize his dedication to his work and his profession; a family portrait to symbolize his love for me and our children; his apron and a tray of cookies to symbolize his hospitality and his love of cooking; a trowel and a bunch of herbs to symbolize his love of gardening and the bounty he transformed into delicious foods; a book entitled *Hugs for Friends* to symbolize the many hugs Al gave through his kindness and concern for others; and lastly, bread and wine to symbolize his faith in God's love and mercy.

I told my children that I had to offer the eulogy at the end. I had to be the one that would tell the world how wonderful this man was and what a loss we were all bearing. Some say they don't know how I did it. "Getting through a funeral takes courage. Friends and family help, but we are still in shock. We still use a buffer of disbelief and vagueness to help us get through this raw phase of grief" (Sanders 49). I just called upon Al to give me the strength.

And so, at the end of the Mass I stood before the entire congregation and offered these words: "Last year I heard a saying on the Oprah show. It was, 'God sends people into our lives for a reason, a season or a lifetime.' I think this aptly sums up Al's mission in life. Some of you knew him only for a very short time, others maybe a decade or more, and still others maybe since he was born. Whatever the time span, there's no doubt that we all lost someone very special to us when Al died the other day. I'm not going to stand here and expound on all his goodness. Your presence here and the presence of those at his wake last night verbalize that more clearly than I ever could. What I do want to say is 'Thank You.' Thank you for making Al the kind of person he was. I firmly believe that he died a much better person than he would have been had you not been a part of his life. And we have to firmly believe that just as he cared about us while he lived that he cares about us in his eternal life, that he's watching over us and is there to soothe us in our pain. During the twelve years since my father's death, I've prayed to him so many times asking for his help in so many matters. My friend Maria reminded me of that the other day when I told her I didn't know what I was going to do without Al. She said to pray to him like I have to my father. And that's what I'm going to suggest all of you do. Pray to Al and talk to him just as you would if he were here.

God sent Al into our lives for a reason, a season or a lifetime. And now God has given us Al the Angel to watch over us until we meet again."

While I don't remember everything about the Mass, the fact that the church was filled with people of all faiths left an impression on me. And as we stood before exiting the church, the recording of Bocelli's song took over. It was only at the end of the song that we proceeded from our seats down the aisles and outside to the cars. From the church we would go directly to the cemetery.

When someone dies in a small town or even in a close-knit community in the city, it is customary for the funeral procession to drive by the house of the departed on its way to the cemetery. Sometimes the cavalcade, led by the hearse, drives by several places that were meaningful to the deceased. This takes the deceased and the mourners on a visit to these significant places one last time in a review of, and a tribute to, the person's life. (Zeitlin and Harlow 154)

Because it would have been backtracking, I didn't request that the cortege pass by our house. This is an omission that I still regret today. Aside from that I really don't recall the ride to the cemetery.

As I had mentioned, there were just a few things that I knew Al wanted when he died. One was that we bring his body to the grave. And because the weather was in our favor, there was a short graveside service rather than one in the cemetery chapel. I had to know that his body was being taken to the right place.

Some of that need stemmed from when my father had died in 1987. It was winter. Taking the body to the grave involved an additional fee, one that was determined to be unnecessary. When I went to visit his grave the next day, I noticed a spray of flowers on it that were not ours, plus they had someone else's name on them. To me that was an indication that my father had not been buried in the proper grave. When I called the cemetery, they said that the workers did not match the flowers to the grave and usually just took flowers from the stand nearby and placed any arrangement once they had filled the grave. However, that uncertainty always bothered me and I know it had bothered Al.

Once when I told a friend about this, she told me that it really didn't make a difference where my father was buried since it was his spirit that lived on. But for me it does make a difference. Unlike others, I do need to visit the graves. I do need that connection. "Rituals are what ground us in our lives, what give us a sense of safety and continuity" (Schraff and Tresniowski 85).

Although it was cold, the sun shone beautifully on Al's casket that day. After the service we headed back home. However, even before we left the cemetery, the workers moved in to lower the coffin. At first I felt like this was so insensitive. When I called and complained about it the next day, the superintendent said it was a hard call. He stated that many people want to see the coffin being lowered to ensure that nothing goes wrong. In retrospect, he was right. After what had happened with my father, this was my assurance that Al was where he was supposed to be.

> Sometimes mourners are encouraged to leave the gravesite before the body is lowered into the grave.

> In other cases, cemeteries have encouraged mourners to perform any last rites and to take leave of the body at a chapel on their grounds, rather than at the gravesite. One can understand some of the motivations behind these practices, such as to allow the cemetery employees to complete their work at their own pace and out of sight of tense mourners, but sending mourners away also distances them from the realities of the death and may run counter to the desired work of making real the implications of the death. (Corr, Nabe, and Corr 281)

I did learn that some of our friends had not followed the funeral cortege and therefore did not know that the service would be graveside. As a result, they waited needlessly at the chapel. It was only after the service was over that they discovered what had transpired—something we should have announced in church.

When we arrived home, the house was filled with people but everything was under control because of my neighbor/friend Donna. It was like a true open house—something Al would have loved. And food was bountiful—something that had always been important to him. In many ways it was not a time of sadness after the funeral. It was more a celebration of his life. I was happy that the children had convinced me to have the collation at home rather than at a restaurant. Al's spirit just seemed to pervade the entire house.

> Death wrenches their physical presence from us; we can no longer share life with them as we once did. But

death does not extinguish our deep desire to cherish them and what we found in life with them....we can fulfill that desire only if we remember. Memory returns them to us in our separation. We can once again see their faces, hear their voices, and love them still. When we actively bring them to mind or reminisce, we can redeem the best of them and our lives together. Only through memory can we consciously acknowledge, explore, appreciate, and cultivate their legacies. (Attig 109-110)

Subsequent Days

The days that followed were easier in some ways. Now I could let down my guard a little, but not completely since I felt I had to maintain a certain calm for the sake of my children. Maybe at that time I was adhering to the modern belief that "grieving was something you did in private, with a minimum of fuss" (Goudge 3).

I had resolved to seek out the doctor whom Al had seen a month before his death when he wasn't feeling well. It had been after our trip to Paris to visit Jenny for Thanksgiving. I thought maybe he had contracted something as a result of the recycled airplane air so often discussed as a factor of illnesses. Al had had all the symptoms of the flu but the doctor did give him medication. And I remember Al saying how he had never felt so sick before. I also recall telling him that he should start getting the flu shot the following year.

But I had to speak to the doctor. Maybe Al had complained to him about something he had kept from me. However, the doctor seemed in disbelief when he read on the chart my reason for being there. He seemed a little distant. I'm not sure if he thought I was looking to place blame and was worried I might sue him. I just wanted to know why my husband had died. "Some philosophers tell us there can be no birth without death, that procreation must preclude immortality, that the earth could not sustain both reproduction and eternally living beings, that we need to clear out and make room for new generations" (Viorst 307).

Why did this man who had never taken blood pressure medication die? Why did this man who took low dose aspirin daily for his heart die of a massive heart attack? The doctor assured me that the blood work done a year before had shown my husband's cholesterol to be within normal range. Was it really as my husband had said so often to me, "When it's your time, it's your time." Maybe that was true but the gnawing question still haunted me—Why now? Why at fifty-four? Why, why, why? "The death precipitates a quest for meaning to make sense out of your loss. You may be among the many grievers who have a profound sense of injustice and disillusionment after the death. You may feel that you have played life by the rules but lost the game" (Rando, *How To* 31).

That evening a colleague called. I was out of school for the remainder of the week so I thought he was calling just to see how I was doing. He had been at the funeral the day before so I wasn't surprised to hear his voice. What did surprise me was the reason behind his call. One of the other teachers, a man in his early fifties like Al, had died that morning. He hadn't been feeling well the day before and had been to the doctor and was supposed to go back that day. When his wife came home midmorning to take him to the appointment, she found him dead. "'But Dorothy's right,' said the Scarecrow. 'No one is exempt from grief'" (Maguire 2).

So within less than a week, two of us had joined the ranks of widowhood. While I'm sure there were many more all around us, these two deaths were so close within our school community. "Because women statistically live longer than men, it is estimated that three out of every four women will be widowed at one time or another" (De Spelder and Strictland 400).

The remainder of the week is a blur. I'm sure we all went through the necessary motions of survival but specifics cannot be recalled. "Most widows agree that during the first days or weeks they are in shock. They act like automatons, often efficiently, viewing their automatic functioning quite objectively, as though they are two people. They have little recollection of events during this early period" (Ginsburg 7).

I planned on going back to school the following Monday. While I probably should have taken off more time, I felt I needed to move forward for my children. Plus it would be a short week since the school was being closed on Wednesday for teachers and students to attend my colleague's funeral. I knew there was no way I could go to the wake or funeral, but I did send a card and note to his wife.

James was scheduled to return to Georgia on Wednesday. That would work out well since I would be able to spend some time with him and bring him to the airport.

And although the new term had begun the week before, Jenny suddenly decided that she didn't want to go back. She asked if she could try to change her schedule and do a co-op locally. I pleaded with her to keep things the way they were. Her room on campus had already been arranged plus her classes were all set. So to help ease the situation she and I agreed that she would commute for a few weeks. "It is clear that major losses such as death do bring disorder...and families must learn to cope with that disruption" (Corr, Nabe, and Corr 229).

The Actual Beginnings of Widowhood

I DON'T THINK THE FACT OF ACTUALLY BEING A widow struck me until a few weeks later, after James had gone back to Georgia and Jenny had decided that commuting to Boston was difficult. I helped her move things into her on-campus apartment one Saturday afternoon in mid-January. But then she came back with me and we spent the rest of the weekend together since it was her birthday. That was difficult, being the lone parent doing all of these things with her.

The Children
by Helen Reichert Lambin

Your children consider themselves half-orphans.
Even if they are young adults now.
Even if they are my children, too.

They grieve together as a family.
But each grieves a separate grief.

One sees in the rose bush all the summers you
were there trimming it—the symbol of
your presence.

One looks for your car in the expressway rush hour,
Going north as you went south—the symbol of
coming home.

One would save every piece of paper you jotted an
idea on—a paper fence to keep the past from escaping.

Together they remember their childhood,
Their father, their bonds.
Going their separate ways to learn
that grief binds us together.
But grief is lived alone.

I tell them I feel half-orphaned, likewise.
But I don't know whether or not they believe me.
Even as they try to do things for me
They think should be done.

But a mother-orphan?
I'm supposed to be the official grown-up now.

Every house should have one.
But how did it get to be me?
(55-56)

I remember that when Jenny left to return to school after the weekend, I called Carlene, a former colleague and dear friend. I cried and told her how much I hated being a widow. "The death of a spouse at any age or stage in life is one of the most emotionally difficult and taxing experiences of anyone's lifetime" (Crenshaw, *Bereavement* 146). Carlene wanted to come over to be with me but I rejected her idea. I had schoolwork that needed to be done. Always the soldier!

Somehow I got through the first month but the end of it came with a horrible "bang"! I received an invitation from the hospital where Al had been brought by the rescue crew. A Mass was being offered for anyone who had died there the previous month. I don't know where my head was but I thought it would be a good idea as opposed to having a private so-called "month's mind" Mass at our church. What a mistake! My daughter came home for it. And my aunt and my mother and some close friends came also. Never did I think that being in that same place where Al had been pronounced dead would have such an overwhelming effect on me. I walked into the chapel and couldn't have been there more than five or ten minutes when I walked out. I began crying and felt I couldn't go back in. I think at that moment the whole realization of Al's death hit me in the face. That composure that I had maintained throughout his funeral was nowhere to be found. I hated that hospital and everything it stood for. To me it wasn't a place of healing; it was a place of death. I remember the priest came out to talk to me. Ironically, it was the same priest who had anointed Al and had been in the room to "tell" me the news. Eventually

I was able to compose myself and I went back into the chapel for the Mass. Aside from visiting my aunt a few years later when she was a patient there and then many years later going to be with a cousin while her mother was being examined in the emergency room, I make it a point not to go to that hospital. Even today I hate even driving by it. As with C. S. Lewis, I could say:

> Tonight all the hells of young grief have opened again; the mad words, the bitter resentment, the fluttering in the stomach, the nightmare reality, the wallowed-in tears. For in grief nothing "stays put." One keeps on emerging from a phase, but it always recurs. Round and Round. Everything repeats. Am I going in circles, or dare I hope I am on a spiral? (66-67)

The following month my son decided to return home from Georgia but wasn't sure if it was a temporary or a permanent move. As a result he left his belongings in storage down there. I think part of him needed to be here out of obligation. He needed to take his father's place and be there for me. It wasn't until later in the year that this notion actually led to a shattering of our relationship. He couldn't stand to see me crying and whenever he did, he told me I needed to see a doctor about medication. I realized later that seeing me in tears made dealing with his father's death all the more difficult for him.

I know much had to do with differences between males and females grieving over a loss. "Women and men often express their reactions to loss and cope with their grief in different ways because they have been socialized to perceive themselves and their roles in different ways" (Corr, Nabe, and Corr 227). Plus I was grieving the loss of a spouse and James was grieving the loss of a parent. "Many people say that a parent's death is one of the hardest things they have ever dealt with in their lives….Any death reminds us of our own mortality, but a parent's death may cause a person to realize, perhaps for the first time, that he or she has become an adult" (DeSpelder and Strictland 395). So actually Al's death was like a double whammy for my son.

Eventually James and I became so angry at each other that we couldn't even have a conversation without it ending in an argument. Once he had permanently moved back home and was established with a new job, I did something that broke my heart. I told him that he would have to move out by the first of the new year, otherwise I was changing the locks on the house. And for the two remaining months he would have to pay me rent. If he went away on business I would prorate his rent, but he would have to pay me to take care of his dog. I don't know who was more in disbelief— he at my saying this or I at actually having said it. In the end James bought his own home, and fortunately, our rocky mother/son relationship was repaired. And yes, all my locks remained intact!

Physicians and Therapists

About a month and a half after Al died, actually the Friday before midwinter school vacation, I went to see my principal about a school matter. It had been a bad day personally, and as I spoke I fell apart. Being a male and young enough to be my son, he probably felt helpless. However, he suggested I speak to the school social worker. Even before I had a chance to seek her out, she appeared at my classroom door and asked if I could stop by to see her before going home that day. And I did.

Rose was very kind. She told me that years before her husband had become seriously ill and she was widowed at the age of thirty-nine. She did remarry four years later. But one of the important things I do remember her saying and have always kept in mind is that eventually I would get to a point when I would say, "What now?" She explained that for her it wasn't only remarrying but also deciding to enter the political field as a councilwoman. She assured me that a day like that would come for me, when I would be able to put my grief aside and make decisions about my future. According to Neimeyer "meaning reconstruction in response to a loss is the central process in grieving" (110). He further emphasizes:

> The reconstruction of a personal world of meaning in the wake of loss must take into account our ongoing relationships with real and symbolic others, as well as the resources of the mourners themselves. Ultimately, we are faced with the task of transforming our identities so as to redefine our symbolic connection to the deceased while maintaining our relationship with the living. (98)

Rose thought that it might be good for me to see a professional to help me deal with my grief. She had the name of a counselor in my town. She did say that she knew nothing about her but that her name was on a list that had been distributed to the schools. I took the number and said I would give it some thought.

I really didn't have to think long since the next day found me an emotional wreck as I looked ahead to a full week off from school. While I had always looked forward to the February break, this year was different. It would give me more time to think about Al.

I must have stared at the counselor's number for a good hour before I dialed it. The person answered and I told her that my husband had died and that I had been given her name by the school social worker. She asked the date of my husband's death. When I told her, she responded, "A month and a half ago? That's good; the wound isn't as raw now."

All I could think was, "Not that raw now? My God, it's so raw I can't stand it." But I said none of this to her. Her words should have been my clue that this woman had no experience as a grief counselor. A counselor maybe, but not for people experiencing a loss. Nevertheless, I agreed to an appointment for the middle of the week.

It wasn't until Tuesday that I really began questioning my decision. As I was driving along I kept thinking of Al and had this feeling that I shouldn't go through with seeing the counselor. Part of me thought it was just the idea of having to talk to a stranger about Al's death. Plus I knew other personal info would have to be discussed as well. However, there was another part of me that was bothered by her insensitive comment about the wound not being as raw now.

> Don't let anyone take your grief away from you. You deserve it, and you must have it. If you had a broken leg, no one would criticize you for using crutches until it healed. If you had major surgery, no one would pressure you to run in a marathon next week. Grief is a major wound. It does not heal overnight. You must have time and the crutches until you can heal. (Manning 65-66)

To this day I think it was Al's intercession that brought about the following. Shortly after I arrived home that evening, there was a phone call for me. It was the counselor. I initially thought she was calling to confirm the appointment the next day. However, it was just the opposite. She was calling to cancel it. She said that they thought her mother-in-law was dying. Then she corrected herself and said that they actually knew she was dying since they had sat all day by her side. She then said that the burial would be out of state so she would not be able to reschedule until she returned since she didn't know how long she'd be away. She said she'd call me when she returned. I said that would be fine.

When I hung up, I sighed a sigh of relief. I couldn't believe it! I knew then that there was no way I'd be going to that individual for help with my grieving process. And several weeks later when she did call, I was happy I wasn't home to get the call. I'm not sure if I called her back. I think I may have called back when I knew the office would be closed and told her I had changed my mind.

That whole experience, as short-lived as it was, is living proof that not all counselors know how to deal with grief, even personally. "Caregivers and professional counselors face their own inevitable losses and it is necessary that they adequately attend to their own grief issues in order to be effective in providing bereavement support and counseling to others" (Crenshaw, "Life Span" 234). So when someone grieving looks for help, it's important to find a professional who is grief sensitive. This concept is stressed by Corr, Nabe, and Corr:

> It is important to note, however, that not all professionals are effective grief counselors. Grief counseling grows out of caring communities, to which it adds formal understanding of experiences in bereavement

and mourning as well as skill in helping individuals with their own coping or problem-solving processes. (256)

But it's not only therapists who need that sensitivity as I discovered seven months later. I hadn't been feeling well; I was actually having some chest pains. "The separation from a loved one may lead to longing sighs, to inertia about everyday activities or to physical symptoms..."(Noppe 5). Consequently, I went to the doctor to be checked out. This was the same doctor that Al had been to a few weeks before he died and to whom I had spoken right after the funeral.

He examined me and found nothing out of the ordinary. However, he did order an EKG to be done immediately. That also showed nothing. But that didn't stop him from looking further. As he explained, women's complaints are always taken lightly by medical professionals so he believed it was necessary to take precautions and investigate further. Consequently he ordered a stress test and a whole series of blood work. And I was encouraged by his attentiveness.

I returned for a follow-up appointment a few weeks later. The doctor told me that the stress test had come back normal. When I asked him about the blood work, he told me everything was perfect including my cholesterol. And I could not believe he said the following, especially since he knew that my husband had died of a heart attack: "With these numbers, you'll never have a heart attack!" My response was that my husband's cholesterol had been good yet he had died of a heart attack. He looked at me and answered a little bit miffed, "Well, you wanted to know the numbers!" His attitude upset me and I began to cry to which he reacted, "Look at you! Nine months and you still can't hold it together." I couldn't believe my ears! I put both palms out for emphasis and said, "Nine months dead and twenty-seven and a half years married! A little inequity there, wouldn't you say. Don't tell me I can't hold it together. From the week after my husband's funeral I have gone into work every day teaching five classes a day. If I stayed home and slept all day, I could understand your reaction. But I have kept going." Evidently, he didn't know that "the death of a husband or wife is a devastating event, one of the most stressful occurrences we face in our lives" (Bouvard 44).

I really can't recall if he apologized, which I tend to doubt. But I walked out of that office that day and resolved never to return to that doctor again. And I didn't!

I do realize that doctors are in the practice of saving lives and sometimes because of their own feelings about death cannot handle situations like mine. However, my experience only proves that the training for all health care professionals but especially doctors needs to include an extensive segment on grief and bereavement. In the beginning of the twenty-first century Holly G. Prigerson and Selby C. Jacobs affirmed that such training was both lacking and needed.

> Despite the frequency with which physicians encounter bereaved patients, medical training offers little guidance in the provision of bereavement ("after") care. Physicians are often uncertain of how to distinguish between normal and pathological grief reactions in their bereaved patients, and how

to manage their health care. Bereavement is associated with declines in health, inappropriate health service use, and increased risk of death. Identifying and intervening on behalf of bereaved patients could help address those increased risks.
(http://jama.ama-assn.org/cgi/content/abstract/286/11/1369)

In the ensuing years, course offerings on death and dying have become more available for undergraduates. But I firmly believe that training in this area must be mandatory for all medical students.

Luckily the year after the above occurrence, I did find a new physician who remains my primary care doctor today. In addition to being highly professional and competent, he is compassionate and concerned for both my physical and emotional well-being.

Busyness

WAS IT THE BUSYNESS OF THOSE FIRST FEW YEARS that kept me from really grieving? As I looked back I knew that had been the case. "Normal or conflicted grief may be delayed for an extended period of time, up to years, especially if there are pressing responsibilities or the mourner feels that he cannot deal with the process at that time" (Rando, "Unresolved Grief" 203).

Back then I really did believe that I was going through the normal grieving process. Yes, I did touch upon each stage as explained by Eizabeth Kubler-Ross: denial, anger, bargaining, depression, and acceptance. Theoretically, a grieving person doesn't necessarily go through the stages in that specific order so I really didn't analyze my process. In hindsight though, I know that I had just skimmed the surface of each stage.

I think my chief concern was trying to maintain an appearance of normalcy for my son and my daughter. "In psychologist William Worden's description of the 'tasks of mourning,'... the third task involves adjusting to a changed environment in which the deceased is missing....The many roles fulfilled by the deceased in the bereaved's life may not be fully recognized until after the loss" (DeSpelder and Strictland 283).

Since Al was an accountant by profession, he had taken care of the finances. I usually described my situation as having been "aware but unaware" of things. So that was really a time-consuming chore that I had to take upon myself. Plus there was so much paperwork to complete as well as legal changes to make as a result of his death.

Keeping up the house and having no one to consult made me weary at times. Yes, there were friends and relatives from whom I could seek advice. However, I got to the point of realizing that I might make mistakes in my decisions; but if I made them I would have no one to blame but myself. I didn't want to put anyone in such a precarious position like that.

PRONOUNS
Then:
We
Our
Ourselves
Ours
Us.
Now:
I
My
Myself
Mine
Me.
Pronouns hurt.
(Lambin 67)

And then there was the lawsuit that had been filed against my husband and the company where he had been employed. One day I received a letter from the lawyer representing them. In it he informed me that the court wanted to know who was the executor of Al's will. That person would be named in his place on the suit. Since I was the executrix of the will, my name would become part of the suit. I was assured it was formality, and that the insurance held by the company would cover any costs incurred. But that didn't make me feel better. It was having to face the fact that even though my husband was dead and not here to defend himself, his reputation was still going to be attacked. And my name was being used instead.

As a result of all this, I think I tread on with the appearance of endurance but later paid a dear price for my bravado.

> How you are as a widow is in large measure shaped and influenced by the attitudes and beliefs of those around you: family, friends, professionals, and the media. How you experience the loss, what you do about it, your pattern of recovery, and who you become are embedded in the world around you. Collectively they reflect the current culture....society's beliefs about widows and widowhood often reflect myths that do not mirror the real experience of widows. These misconceptions and half-truths can interfere with recovery and with personal development. (Lieberman 206)

A Cry for Help

It wasn't until the latter part of 2001, months after my daughter had graduated from college, that I truly began to think about my life without Al. I wasn't sure just what I needed but I began to think that maybe belonging to a widows/widowers group would be helpful. I sought the help of a priest where I was attending services at the time. I made my request through a phone call which was never actually answered by him personally. Instead, I received a call from an individual who was in charge of outreach programs. She told me that my name had been referred to her and she asked me to come in to discuss my suggestion.

I sat down with her one afternoon. She scribbled notes while I told her that I believed that some type of group open to widows and widowers would be beneficial. My intention was not to have a totally social group but one where individuals experiencing the loss of a spouse could come together to talk and share feelings about their grief. I specifically remember her asking me if I thought that one of the purposes of the group would be matchmaking. No! That definitely was not my intention although I reiterated that having some social events for the group would be advantageous. I remember that it was November when I met with her. As I left she told me she would type up a proposal, and then forward it to me to see if it presented my ideas appropriately.

The holidays came and went as well as Al's second anniversary. Nothing came in the mail. I remember telephoning this woman in January to ask about the proposal. She apologized and said that she had been busy, but would work on it and get it out to me.

When I saw her around Easter, all she said was hello, and then asked me how I was doing. I was frustrated that she had made no mention of my idea for a support group. I had always been a person to speak up when not satisfied, but here I was speechless. I was going to report the situation to the priest I had initially contacted, but what would I say? That one of his workers hadn't done her job? And shortly afterwards, that priest announced that he would be leaving for another assignment. In some ways I looked upon this as a plus. But on second thought, I knew running to his replacement about unaccomplished things would not prove to be good in the end.

I sometimes think that this lack of support was a type of disenfranchised grief. "Grievers are disenfranchised when they are not recognized by society as persons who are entitled to experience grief or who have a need to mourn" (Corr, Nabe, and Corr 245). For whatever reason, this woman's failure to help me made me feel so alone and abandoned. And consequently, I found myself turning away from this haven where I had initially sought refuge after Al's death.

"One of the profoundly disturbing consequences of disenfranchised grief is that because of a lack of social sanctioning and social support, the bereaved may become disillusioned with and alienated from their community" (Kauffman 20).

And so the months passed and I could see myself getting worse; "...disenfranchising circumstances can intensify feelings of anger, guilt and powerlessness" (Doka 7). I realized afterwards that although I had gone through all the motions of grieving, deep down I had not fully faced all my demons. I had always let the busyness of life prevent me from fully facing Al's death and the consequences of it. "The problem of disenfranchised grief can be expressed in a paradox. The very nature of disenfranchised grief creates additional problems for grief, while removing or minimizing sources of support" (Doka 7).

I finally called my friend Carlene and asked her if she knew of anyone I could go to for help. I knew I had finally reached the stage where a support group alone was not going to help. She told me she would contact a friend of hers and get me a name.

And as promised, within a few days Carlene called with the name of an individual at a local hospice organization. While she didn't know the person herself, one of her friends had heard her speak to a group and believed she could be helpful to me. I immediately called Julia and spoke to her a few minutes on the phone, just enough time to tell her my situation and to make an appointment with her.

The following week I made the thirty-mile trip to see her. To a Rhode Islander that is a voyage! Although I was very nervous, Julia immediately put me at ease as I told her "my story." And then she told me hers. She had been widowed twice—once after a long-term illness and the second suddenly, like my situation. And she not only survived it all but was now helping others who were grieving. "A widow's grief can be incomprehensible to anyone other than another widow. The death of a spouse is more than a loss; it is the end of a way of life that survived the good and bad experiences and emotions" (Peabody and Mooney 23).

Julia said that she could tell I was depressed and needed to see a professional. She gave me the names of several people. She noted that it was important to see someone who was trained in grief therapy. "Finding a good counselor to help you through the grief process sometimes takes a little doing" (Wolfelt, *How To* 13). She also thought it might be helpful for me to be part of a grief support group that she would be starting at the end of January. She told me to keep it in mind. Deep down inside I knew I was long overdue for all of this!

> Here is what I would tell survivors. Allow yourself to mourn at your own pace, but seek out a support group when you feel you are ready....The ongoing struggles with fear, guilty thoughts, angry, raging outbursts may indicate that you need professional attention especially if these persist six or more months after the sudden death experience. (Hersh 24)

And so I began my journey of recovery by making a few phone calls. One of the therapists on the card called me back. My answers to her questions amounted to an abbreviated version of "my story." When I finished she asked me if I had questions to ask her. No one had ever said that to me before. I was actually allowed to question a professional! I really can't recall the questions I asked her aside from how long she had been working in the field of grief therapy. After a few moments she told me we could meet for an appointment and then decide if we were a match. That "if" caught me off guard. Again, something new! Having an appointment with her did not automatically mean that I would continue seeing her on a regular basis. I would have a choice; and she would have a say in the choice as well! What a novel concept! "Trust your instincts. You may leave your first counseling session feeling like you have clicked with your counselor. On the other hand, it may take you several sessions to form an opinion" (Wolfelt, *How To* 15).

Road to Recovery

My first appointment was scheduled for the week before Christmas. In some ways that was good. Al had always loved the holidays and they had not been the best of times for me since his death. I was nervous but Patricia seemed to put me at ease. I remember crying and then feeling like a load had been lifted off my shoulders. I needed someone to listen to me talk about Al without feeling uncomfortable with my sadness.

> Memory brings aspects of the past into present awareness. When we remember those we love, we reconnect with them even as we continue in new and unexpected directions. This connection is fragile when compared to connection in their presence—but it is nevertheless substantial and precious.
>
> Conscious remembering and shared reminiscing enrich our present living. And they enable us to carry much of lasting value into the future. Memory allows us to reclaim and revive our appreciation of those we

still love and the gifts they continue to give us. We can cherish their legacies here and now. We take delight in having known them and loved them. As we cherish them, we experience again the praise, gratitude and joy they bring to our hearts. (Attig 111)

Patricia skipped the following week but scheduled an appointment for the day before Al's third anniversary. At that meeting she asked what I was going to do the next day. She thought it was necessary for me to have a plan and not leave the day to chance.

The next day I went over to my daughter's apartment to hang some curtains I had made for her. But first we went out for a bite to eat. Spending time with Jenny was good. It made me feel close to Al since she was a result of his love for me and mine for him. Plus it got me through the time frame of that afternoon that tends to be a concentration with me.

Later, I decided to stop by my mother's and go to New Year's Eve Mass with her. I realized later that this idea had been a mistake. Being in the church where Al and I had been married flooded me with too many memories I wasn't ready for. Looking back I think I could identify with Joan Didion's feelings regarding memories when she wrote *Blue Nights*. "'You have your wonderful memories,' people said later, as if memories were solace. Memories are not. Memories are by definition of times past, things gone.... Memories are what you no longer want to remember" (64).

Then I found it wasn't good to see people I knew, especially couples. Over the years I came to realize that a perfectly normal reaction to seeing married couples my age together is jealousy. Why me and not them? What clout did they have that they still had each other? Sad to say that at some points I even felt that way about close friends. "When death takes a midlife spouse there may be feelings of tremendous outrage that both the deceased mate and the surviving spouse have been cheated out of their hard-earned reward of an easier life following the struggle to raise a family, establish a career, and assume economic security" (Crenshaw, *Bereavement* 146-147).

But I think part of those "ill" feelings came as a result of the overall stigma of being a widow and people's reactions to that word. One of the characters in Elizabeth Strout's book entitled *Olive Kitteridge* senses that attitude from one of her friends. "...But now it was as though she'd won a lottery because he was still alive, and Olive thought Bunny could see what it was like, her friends losing their husbands and drowning in emptiness. In fact, Bunny—Olive sometimes thought—didn't really want to be around Olive too much, as though Olive's widowhood was like a contagious disease" (256-257).

Afterwards I went home and somehow survived the night and the next day. But it's amazing how I have relived those days surrounding Al's death and somehow still feel the pain every now and then.

Life definitely changes with a death. I had seen that before with the death of my father and then with the deaths of Al's parents, and more recently with the death of my mother eight years ago. Customs and traditions are affected. And no matter the effort to maintain them, they're never the same. The key to survival is to hold on to the ones that can be maintained even with some alterations, but also begin new ones. And that's not always easy to do. "Facing change is one of the hardest lessons of grief" (Sanders 200-201).

I continued to see Patricia on a weekly basis. There was always a sense of relief when I would walk out of her office. It was like a purging of all that was keeping me from feeling better. Towards the end of January I began a six-week support group facilitated by Julia from hospice. So there was a period of time when I was doing double duty in dealing with my grief—one day with Patricia and the other with the group. I never felt it was too much; I actually looked forward in a different way to each experience.

I was very nervous on the first day of group. Foremost, I wasn't sure if I had the right place. I arrived early to make sure I could find it. I basically waited in the car until I saw others emerge from their vehicles. As soon as I saw Julia, I felt "safe." The group was made up of individuals, all of whom had suffered various losses during the previous months. I think the longest was six months, aside from me with three years. That fact caught everyone by surprise. My husband had died three years before and here I was just now entering a support group! I tried to explain to the group the reason for my delay. That up until a year before I had always thought I had faced my grief head-on but came to realize that I had barely scratched the surface. They seemed to understand what I said and I think they felt bad for me. But whatever their feelings, I felt comfortable being there—willing to share and willing to listen to their sharing as well. "They (bereavement support group members) attend to learn to live in a world from which their loved one is missing. They want to give and receive support...." (Hughes 183).

The group was an all-female one. In some ways I was happy about that. I think we could be more open and emotional if we wanted. "Wolfelt (1990) sees men's grief as naturally complicated because of difficulty in overcoming their social conditioning to repress their feelings. They need to appear self-sufficient, cannot let themselves appear nonproductive, and cannot ask for help" (Hughes 5).

Each session lasted about two hours and Julia adhered to that schedule. I think when there are suffering souls together in one place, there has to be a time limit; otherwise they can go on forever. "Ending sessions on time can be difficult, since members may need and want more time and because the expression of such intense emotion is difficult to conclude on cue" (Cook and Dworkin 107).

There were several widows—all married from maybe ten years to about forty. But it wasn't just from them that I drew comfort—the ones who were enduring the loss of a parent brought back memories of my own father's death. My dad became ill in November 1987 and died three days after Christmas as a result of pancreatic cancer. He had been sick only a month and a half. I had always thought about my father after he died. But once Al died it seemed my grief over my husband's death consumed me. I seemed only to concentrate on that. Losing a parent and losing a spouse..."That is why a man leaves his father and mother and clings to his wife, and the two of them become one body" (Genesis 2:24). Maybe that's why Al's death seemed to have overtaken me. A part of me had been taken away!

One session in particular seems to stand out in my memory. That was the week we were asked to bring in pictures of the person whose death had brought us together. It was like putting a face to a name. Before that we all could empathize and offer our support, but seeing a face for each name made such a difference. "So that's why you're so sad" seemed like the words I wanted to express.

I looked forward to the group each week and as the time for the last meeting approached, I felt a little saddened. I think it was because I was spending time with people who knew how I was feeling as I understood how they were feeling. I felt safe talking about my sadness and my loss. I could also see how dependent one can become on others. Hence, the reason these groups are run for a limited time only. In his guide for bereavement support groups, Alan Wolfelt cautions:

> Many grief support groups are so successful they resist ending. However, "graduation" from the support group is an important step toward reconciliation of the death of someone.
>
> Expect a certain amount of ambiguity of feelings about the ending of the group. Ending may elicit withdrawal in some, sadness in others, and happiness yet in others. (*The Understanding* 39-40)

I also came to realize that timing is so important. Had I attempted to join a group a month and a half after my husband had died at the suggestion of my son, I know it wouldn't have worked. I was, in a sense, "ripe" for it three years later. Plus I believe in happenings being providential. To me this delayed part of my journey was meant to take place at the time it did.

When the support group did come to an end, the participants talked about staying in touch. I did attempt to have a get-together. A few attended; but there was no discussion of future gatherings.

Over the years I would sometimes think about the other members of that group and wonder how they were doing, especially the widows. Did they still miss their husbands like I missed mine? Did they have a new person in their lives? Had they remarried?

To this day I have maintained contact with one other widow in the group. Holly and I talk or communicate via texting or mail, and try to get together once in a while. She used to tell me how she was a little surprised when she heard me tell the group back then that it had been three years since my husband had died. She recalled telling herself that would never be the case with her, still grieving so actively after that number of years. But later Holly did understand that a person can't predict the length of time for grieving when she realized that her grief was a complicated one, colored by so many factors in her life. "For many, current loss brings to the surface unresolved grief from the past, thus adding an element to the healing process that complicates and prolongs grief work" (Cook and Dworkin 100). And sometimes I wonder if she was ready for that particular group since it had been less than three months since her husband's death. I know at times she couldn't even speak and found it very difficult to share with everyone. But maybe just listening to others was helpful for her. Maybe hearing others talk about their loss and their sorrow carried her through those first months. Plus had Holly not been a part of that group, we would never have met. It goes back to the quote I used at Al's funeral. "People come into our lives for a reason, a season or a lifetime."

And while I no longer had the support group, I still had Patricia. Sometimes it seemed like I was going nowhere. I would always be examining the same feelings, the same regrets, the same questions. In retrospect, I think maybe I was expecting too much from myself, especially because it had been over three years since Al's death. I am impatient by nature; but I had to learn to be patient with myself and the journey I was taking. As Antoine De Saint-Exupéry states, "It is idle, having planted an acorn in the morning, to expect that afternoon to sit in the shade of the oak" (45).

I saw Patricia weekly for most of that first year. Towards the end of it I switched to every other week depending on how I was feeling. Patricia let me set the pace. However, my connection did not stop after a year or even two years. It continued on occasion until her relocation/retirement. Every so often when the clouds and barrenness of winter would get to be too much for me to handle, I would give her a call. Sometimes it was around a holiday or a special anniversary. Sometimes it was a one-time visit; other times it flowed into two or maybe three. "Some bereaved people only need a few sessions, while others benefit from a longer-term counseling relationship" (Wolfelt, *How To* 22).

Several years later after I was no longer seeing Patricia,

my primary care physician thought it would probably be a good idea for me to seek professional help once again. Some family matters I was dealing with were in turn affecting some residual grief. As a result Ellie entered my life, and to this day she continues to provide "oil changes" as I comically refer to our occasional sessions. Some might look upon this dependency on counseling as a negative. On the contrary; it's recognizing the need to seek help when the occasion arises.

I know I have definitely changed since that first counseling session back in December of 2002 and the years since then. And that's a good thing! But the one thing I know will never change is Al forever having a place in my heart. And that's not so bad either!

> The widowed person's relationship with the deceased spouse includes strong themes of letting go and holding on. These two themes are intertwined and not polar opposites....
>
> Within the context of letting go, there is holding on to the tie with the deceased. Memory provides the major link between the widowed person and the deceased spouse. Memory holds together past and present and gives continuity to human life. Nostalgia and sentimentality about the past heighten the impact of recollections. (Moss and Moss 165)

My "Blue" Room

It was probably more than halfway through my first year of seeing Patricia that I made a discovery about myself. It came as a result of reading a book by Phyllis Greene, a fellow widow, entitled *It Must Have Been Moonglow*. She called the last chapter in her book "The Blue Room." She began by actually reiterating the thoughts I had had and continued to have at times:

> My husband died more than two years ago. Sometimes it feels as if ten years have passed and sometimes it feels like last week. So much has happened in the world around me, and actually the changes in me are astonishing. I have made the first steps in the journey of widowhood, and I think I am stronger and as self-reliant as I had expected to be. I am used to my own company much of the time, and I'm not too bad a companion to be around. I accept who I am and I can handle it. Amen. (157)

As part of her personal makeover, Mrs. Greene converted a sitting room into a more modern computer/TV room. She decorated it to her own liking and adorned it with not only memories of her husband but also of her entire family. It seemed to symbolize her transformation that she spoke about in the above quote. She ended the chapter by saying, "My only hope for those of you who read this is that your loneliness and sorrow will abate (it never goes away), and that you will soon be on your way to creating a Blue Room of your own" (160).

In September of 2003 I decided to clean up my son's former bedroom and make it into a room where I could go to read and relax and listen to music. My room had to be bright to survive those gloomy days of winter. When I initially showed James and Jenny the color I wanted to paint the walls, they talked me out of it. They suggested a toned-down color called "lemon sorbet." One coat on the walls had me puckering my lips and voting for the second coat to be my first choice color, "sunflower yellow."

Over the years some of the items in that room changed but the color remained the same. On one wall hung hats that represented my parents, my in-laws, my children and their spouses, my husband and myself. Handprints from my grandchildren were added to the wall after their births. On another wall were the papal blessings from our marriage, my parents' twenty-fifth anniversary, and Al's parents' twenty-fifth anniversary. Still another wall held a framed print of irises given to Al and me by our children, their first joint Christmas gift to us so long ago. And the "window" wall held a painting my daughter did when she first embarked on her journey as a "budding" artist, and my certificates in thanatology, one from Mount Ida College and the other from the Association for Death Education and Counseling. My room also included a bookshelf, and my dad's old recliner as well as a cricket chair which my parents had given me on my seventh birthday. A treadle sewing machine and a small table served as platforms for numerous meaningful knickknacks and pictures. A boom box sat on top of the bookshelf ready to play some of Al's favorite music as well as music that I alone had come to enjoy during my years as a widow. Near the door were two suitcases that acted as storage containers but served to bring back some wonderful memories. Those American Touristers were our first "couple suitcases." Al had purchased them before we were married and we took them on our honeymoon. And lastly, on the bookshelf along with many favorite books were pictures of Al and the spouses of friends who had joined this strange organization called widowhood.

But there was always remembrance, not sadness, when I used to sit in that room of warmth and color. It served as a haven when the dreariness of winter would overcome me, and acted like a security blanket when I became frightened. But above all it acted as a symbol that I was continually moving forward because like Phyllis Greene I had created my own "Blue Room," a place to sit and ponder and remember. "As we remember and cherish stories of those who have died, we sustain our connection with them. We hold them dear as we welcome differences they still make in our lives. We retain and appreciate the gifts that were their lives. We give their legacies places in our hearts—and, in this way, become their living legacies" (Attig 53).

When Phyllis Greene died in 2011, I felt like I had lost a true friend. Her death made me sad. She had been such an inspiration to me and that I found truly amazing. She was in her early eighties when she wrote her book, yet I could identify with her in spite of our age difference. I remember e-mailing her and telling her about Al's death, and how and what I was feeling. In response she wrote:

> Thank you for writing your thoughtful and candid letter. I am humbled and honored that you felt that you wanted to share your feelings with me.
>
> Widowhood is a hard road and a strange journey—but we are on it together. I understand everything that you say and, the sad part is that there are so many of us in this overcrowded, sad boat. But we can all try to persevere with joy...and keep trying and keep trying...and I send all good wishes. Phyllis Greene

Tears

It was always amazing how the tears could come so easily at times. I could be fine one moment and then crying, sometimes uncontrollably, the next. Occasionally I could almost anticipate the tears and then at other times I could not predict that it would happen.

> But the truth is that few people ever feel completely finished with mourning. Some feelings and issues may always remain. This is probably not reassuring to a mourner who expects that the formal end of bereavement means the complete absence of pain. But that kind of healing is likely also to mean the absence of memory and would ultimately negate the relationship that the mourner had with the deceased. To lose our capacity to be moved, touched and to remember would betray the person who died and the significance of our relationship with him or her. Ultimately, it would betray ourselves. (Brenner 209)

In the beginning I suppose it's expected and almost a natural thing. I remember the first time I went to the bank a few days after Al had died. I began to ask the teller a question about one of the accounts and midway through the sentence I choked up and cried. I felt ashamed and excused myself and explained that my husband had recently died.

And then a few months later when I received an insurance check, I looked at it and cried. I didn't consider myself fortunate to have the money to cover some expenses. Rather I looked upon it as "blood money."

But there were other times over the years when tears have been not only for the sadness of Al's death but also for the future he never had.

> A person spends years coming into his own, developing his talent, his unique gifts, perfecting his discriminations about the world, broadening and sharpening his appetite, learning to hear the disappointments of life, becoming mature, seasoned—finally a unique creature in nature, standing with some dignity and mobility and transcending the animal condition; no longer driven, no longer a complete reflex, not stamped out of any mold. And then the real tragedy, as André Malraux wrote in *The Human Condition*: that it takes sixty years of incredible suffering and effort to make such an individual, and then he is good only for dying. (Becker 268-269)

At my daughter's college graduation I seemed to be okay. And then I found out she had decorated her mortarboard with her father's funeral prayer card. That brought me to tears. It was the realization that although she rarely talked about his death, she missed him and wanted him close on that special day.

Even the market could be a bad place for me. Seeing items on sale like Lay's potato chips or Thomas's English muffins, my husband's favorites, could cause me to put on dark glasses to hide the tears from other shoppers.

And then there was the time when I went to France to celebrate turning sixty. I had thought the day of our wedding anniversary would be a tough one. Maybe because I geared myself up for it, it actually turned out to be a wonderful day. I walked along a street ironically bearing the Boulet name. I stopped and bought myself a bouquet of roses, the same color as the ones my maids had carried at our wedding. Later I had lunch at a little café nearby. All the while I had Al on my mind, but in a happy way by remembering our wedding day thirty-four years before.

But the tears did come on my last full day in Paris. I was walking along the Left Bank near the university where my daughter had spent the months before her father's death. And I became so, so sad. I thought of how terrible it was that she would come back to the States and within twelve days of her return face her father's death.

Watching a movie or even the news showing a happy family could move me to tears. I think it was because I knew that although I had my family, and they had me, the most important link in our circle of love was missing.

And as I grew older, I would feel the loss of Al even more and at times felt lonely. But Edgar Jackson puts that emotion in perspective for me with his following explanation:

> The loneliness that is so important a part of the complex emotion of grief must be appreciated for what it is if it is to be managed wisely. It is evidence of the empty spot in life that has been left by someone's death. It is verification of the importance of that other person to life. It is a response of life to the loss of the object of love. It is a diminishing of the experience of life because the life that was shared can no longer be shared in the same way. (34)

People would often tell me that enough time had passed, that I should be dating and looking for someone to share the rest of my life with. However, I think of the advice that was given to Dr. Joyce Brothers after her husband had died. "'Don't fall into the trap of marrying just because you are lonely. You will be lonelier than ever. Marriage is not the magic cure-all. Love is what makes the difference'" (163).

And deep down inside I didn't want someone else; I just wanted Al. And the fact that I couldn't have him would make me sometimes cry even many years later. And that's okay!

> In marriage one partner—unless both are killed simultaneously—must go before the other. Usually the man goes first. Generations of wives have known this. Now I knew it too, and must adapt. I must force myself to look upon the familiar things, the coat hanging on the chair, the hat in the hall, the motoring gloves, the stick, the pile of yachting magazines beside his bed, and remind myself that this was not

a separation of war that we had known twenty years earlier, but separation for all time....I wept often because I could not prevent the tears, and possibly, in some way beyond my understanding, tears helped the healing process.... (du Maurier 150, 151)

Secondary Losses

"As a griever you must cope with secondary losses. These are the physical and/or symbolic losses that develop as a consequence of the death of the person you loved" (Rando, *How To* 15). I sometimes think that my need for counseling has been especially stronger when a secondary loss comes into the picture. And those can keep coming for as long as I live. Rando notes that "simply because they are secondary does not mean they are insignificant; frequently they are harder to resolve than the initial loss" (*How To* 252). When a death occurs, people don't initially realize that they are losing not only the special individual but also all their hopes and dreams for the future.

Al used to always say he hoped one day to open a small restaurant for breakfast and lunch after he retired. I may have even pictured the two of us working alongside each other. I guess I just assumed we'd grow old together.

But the secondary losses from Al's death have not been limited to me alone. Both my children have had to deal with them as well. Al has not been there to cheer them for their accomplishments, and to comfort and support them in their low moments. Most especially, Al wasn't there to walk Jenny down the aisle when she was married in 2009. But from the smile on her face as she walked alone, I could tell she knew her dad was with her.

The secondary losses have continued with the births of our grandchildren, Kendra, Patrick, and Nicholas. Al is not here to enjoy them with me, and to watch them grow and develop. But the three of them are also losing out by not having their grandfather here to spend time with them and marvel at all their achievements both big and small.

Throughout the years since Al's death I have come to realize that each secondary loss has to be mourned, some more than others. It would probably be easier to cast them aside and forget about them, and concentrate on the joys surrounding some of them. But I am convinced that everything is intertwined, just like the joy of having had Al in my life and the sorrow of losing him.

> When you are joyous, look deep into your heart and you will find it is only that which has given you sorrow that is giving you joy.
> When you are sorrowful look again in your heart, and you will see that in truth you are weeping for that which has been your delight.
> Some of you say, "Joy is greater than sorrow," and others say, "Nay sorrow is greater."
> But I say unto you, they are inseparable. (Gibran 29-30)

Feeling His Presence

Al always enjoyed cooking. I was told that even as a young child he loved watching and helping his mother or his grandmother in the kitchen. And it was a good thing since my cooking skills were limited when we first got married. Actually, I think from the very start they were improved by Al's lead. And, in most instances, they were more than complemented by Al's expertise, especially on holidays. I would do all the trimmings and the running around for the ingredients, and the rest was Al's job, or should I say pleasure.

In the first year of going to Patricia, I remember her telling me to focus on what Al had given me through our marriage. At first I didn't quite understand what she meant. Then she explained with an example from her own life. She told me she had gained a great appreciation for theatre through her husband. After that I really didn't have to think very long before I answered "Cooking and baking."

As mentioned above I really hadn't done much cooking when I lived at home so my culinary skills were really at a minimum. And I have to truthfully say that I never enjoyed cooking and always looked forward to Al taking over that chore on the weekends and holidays. However, the one thing I did enjoy was baking Christmas cookies with him. We each had our own favorites and together we made up beautiful trays to be presented to friends, relatives, and coworkers. My mother would often say that Al and I should start a business since our creations always looked so professional.

The year he died, Al simplified his part of our cookie making enterprise with a purchase he made. He had always wanted one of those professional heavy-duty Kitchen Aid mixers but the cost prevented it from being a priority. However, that changed in February, 1999. I will never forget his phone call that day when he told me the mixers were on sale and he was going to stop to buy one. Unfortunately, not all stores had them in stock but he did locate one at a mall in the neighboring state where he worked. When he came home with this monstrosity, I just shook my head in disbelief! However, he was like a kid who had just experienced an early Christmas.

Al loved the mixer and always found an excuse to use it; he never seemed to tire of "his toy." And so the December before he died found me mixing my recipes by hand and Al using his "beast" as we did our usual cookie co-baking,

After my husband died, the mixer basically stayed in its place in a lower cupboard. At times I thought it had been such a waste since Al hadn't even gotten to use it a full year. And there was no way I was about to consider using it.

Then one day I looked at it and decided to put it on the counter. I looked at the booklet of directions with no intention of committing to using it. But just seeing it there in the open flooded me with such wonderful memories of my husband. And so, I made an attempt to try it out. And that attempt led to another and to another. Now I don't know what I would do without it. I can honestly say that I have come to love "the beast." And over the years I have realized that I would never have gone out to buy this mixer for myself so in a sense I look upon it as a gift from Al.

And the place in the house that I never really cared about before has become a source of peace. It is in my kitchen where I always feel my husband's presence especially when I am cooking or baking, tasks that never were my forte. I now look upon them as a legacy my husband has left.

> Although people in western cultures are accustomed to thinking of themselves as "individuals," proud of their distinctiveness from others, in fact we all represent "pastiche personalities," reflecting characteristics modeled on an enormous range of persons who have been important to us. Without really intending it, from our very first days of life we appropriate ways of gesturing, thinking, speaking, feeling, and acting from our parents, relatives, friends, and even public figures with whom we identify. In a sense, then, we become living memorials to these persons, even after they themselves have died. Noting the imprint that such people have made on our own lives can be a powerful way of honoring their contribution, forming a living web of connection that we, through our lives, extend to others. (Neimeyer 149)

But that "living web of connection" doesn't rest only with me, because my children have truly inherited their father's culinary skills. Like my husband, James doesn't always rely on recipes. He can put together a meal based upon what he has on hand. And seasoning is contingent upon taste, not measurement. He wastes nothing. His soups can contain anything and everything. He also believes homemade pasta sauce (aka gravy) has to simmer for hours to be good, something he remembers from when his father used to make it.

Jenny is more of a recipe person. But I am so impressed by the things she attempts. When she went to a farmers' market one day, she received a bonus ball of smoked mozzarella with her purchase. She went home, checked the internet, and found a great pasta recipe that included the cheese. On another occasion she found a recipe for lentil soup that called for parsnips. I probably would have just left them out, but not my daughter. As a result she educated me as to what they are.

So what about the beast that still resides in my kitchen? Since Jenny has a smaller version of it, maybe James will want it. Otherwise, I'm hoping Kendra or one of my grandsons will take it. After all, I want my legacy and my husband's staying in the kitchen. I just don't want it going into the dumpster placed under my deck after I die.

Pennies from Heaven

For longer than I can remember, each night when Al would change from his work clothes, he had his little routine of emptying his pockets. He would put his keys, wallet, and his rosary case on the cedar chest next to his side of the bed. Then he would check his change. He would remove any pennies and place them in a leather cup on his dresser. The rest of the change would go next to his wallet for his coffee the next morning. When the penny cup was filled, he would empty it into a big jar; and as the need arose we would roll the coins and turn them in at the bank for dollar bills.

Shortly after Al died I began finding pennies all over the house. At first I really didn't pay much attention to it. Later I came to realize that they would show up at times when I needed Al the most. And after a while I began to hold on to those coins and referred to them as "pennies from heaven."

One morning I was lying in bed and having a very difficult time motivating myself to get up. It was a "down" moment when I was missing Al so much. When I went to roll over, there was a penny by my side. I think it was Al telling me to get up and go on.

Over the years situations like this have happened frequently. However, there have been long lapses without them, when I really haven't given the absence of them any thought. I guess it's at those times that Al feels I'm doing okay on my own.

There was one time at church when I was feeling sad and missing him very much. I happened to put my hand in my pocket and there was a penny. Now some skeptics might say it was leftover change from another time. Maybe yes, and maybe no. For me it was Al speaking. "ADC (After Death Communication) signs provide much hope to those that are grieving deeply, especially bereaved parents and the widowed. But because they are a symbolic form of communication, the receiver must interpret his or her own experience and assign personal meaning to it" (Guggenheim and Guggenheim 211).

Years ago the father of a friend died after an illness. On the morning of the funeral I was thinking of Al. It had been a while since I had received a penny. I went down to iron something to wear and there on the ironing board was a copper coin. I immediately felt I needed to share it with my friend's mother. So I gave it to her later and recounted my story. I told her that I thought the coin was meant for her, to let her know that her husband would be there for her like Al had continued to be there for me. She smiled and thanked me, and said that she probably would be finding quarters since that's what her husband used to save.

Now the amusing and strange part of this story is that I

began finding quarters in my house following that funeral. And unbeknownst to me, my friend's mother was finding pennies all over. When we shared our stories, we laughed and told our husbands they had this whole thing mixed up. The pennies were for me and the quarters belonged to her. I think this showed us that even in death there can be humor as our loved ones continue to communicate with us. Eventually the right coins showed up at the right house.

And to this day I am still surprised when a penny seems to come just at the right moment, when I need a reminder from Al that he's always with me.

Going It Alone

Phyllis Greene described her oneness with her husband so well when she stated:

> I always have and always will think of myself as Phyllis and Bob....Just as our names so comfortably sound like one person, so did our very being. We were so much of a mind that, from another room, I could ask or comment or suggest almost anything on any subject, and Bob would have been thinking of the same thing. It was a phenomenon because it happened so often without a common reminder that might have led us to the subject. (66-67)

And so it was with Al and me. AlandAnn, AnnandAl. Two hearts meshed into one being. That was not to say that we were the same. Far from it! Al was an Aries and I a Cancer. It has been noted in astrology books that these two signs are not the most compatible. A relationship is possible but has to be worked at. And such was ours. And I would never trade those rough times for anything else. I think it was the mingling of our different personalities that made us a couple.

But after Al's death I found it was solely Ann. There was no one to be thinking my thoughts or ready to speak the same words. Moreover, there was no one to share the joys and the sorrows, the doubts and the assurances.

About a month before Al died, we visited our daughter in Paris. One evening my fast gait got the best of him, especially when I proceeded along a side street without him. When I slowed down and rejoined him, he commented that I would never do well in cultures where women traditionally follow the men. I knew he was joking but I often wondered if somehow Al had had a premonition of his death and saw my role as a widow. And in a sense without my realizing it, he was telling me I'd be all right when he died.

So while I learned to be independent and walk alone, I did it strictly out of necessity. It's not a role I relished. Eventually, however, I became comfortable with this new persona knowing Al had somehow been part of this transformation.

No One Ahead of Me

No one ahead of me on the
front line, standing before
the fire, willing to be
consumed to give me life
No larger shadow daunting
me, no one to emulate
or to disdain…Now
I can look: there's
nothing to deflect or
mask my vision. On
the far side of the
chasm is the place
where you have gone.
For the first time,
you will not reach
out to save me.
(Rapoport 22)

Mission in Life

At some point while on my "road to recovery," Rose's question popped up before me. "What now?" I began to think about what I wanted to do with the rest of my life. I realized that my teacher personality would prevail even after I would leave the field of education. And I felt strongly about doing something that would make Al's death serve a purpose.

I'm not certain how or when, but the idea of "aftercare" came up and sparked my interest.

> Aftercare can be defined as a means of helping survivors cope after the loss of a loved one. In today's fast-paced, high tech, and extremely mobile society, the family and social systems that previously provided emotional and physical support are not present as they were a generation ago....In response to that unmet need, some funeral homes are now offering "Aftercare" programs for their clients and community members. (Miletich 25)

I think individuals establish such a close relationship, almost an "intimacy," with a funeral home during a very personal time in their lives. And from experience I can attest to that. And then after the funeral, it's over! When someone has been ill and dies, there's usually some connection with a hospice organization that continues afterwards. But not so with a sudden death.

> Funeral homes must be leaders in providing aftercare. It is a natural extension of the care that they provided leading up to and including disposal of the body and death rituals. Because funeral home staff members are seen as helpful, they would have little difficulty maintaining positive relationships with the bereaved. Thus, they are the natural choices to provide aftercare services. (Johnson and Weeks 6)

In the fall of 2003 before pursuing some studies for this new venture, I began volunteering at the funeral home that had arranged Al's services. I thought it would be wise to see if I could handle being in that environment on a regular basis.

It was interesting to see the reactions of people I knew when they would encounter me there. When I tried to explain what I was thinking of doing, some responded by saying that it was a great idea if that was going to help me through my grief. But that wasn't the purpose at all! I was doing this as a result of my grief. And not many people could understand it; and that was okay.

Through some networking I was given the name of a woman in the field of aftercare on the West Coast. So I contacted Catherine. She told me I would be a hard sell and that funeral homes normally don't see the value in someone who is not an immediate moneymaker for them. Her words did not deter me, but I always kept them in the back of my mind. Consequently, by the end of 2007 I became Certified in Thanatology (CT) by the Association for Death Education and Counseling, and the following year I received a Certificate in Thanatology from Mount Ida College.

My original plan was to seek a position with a funeral home, and have everything all set up before retiring from teaching. But it didn't work out that way. In the summer of 2010 I found myself ready to leave my career in education, a little earlier than I had thought. But I knew I was doing the right thing. As Fahy states in her book *A Time for Leaving*, "If the Leaving is truly right....you will be at peace" (58). And peace definitely replaced the burden of deciding!

While the concept of Funeral Home Aftercare has been around for a while, unfortunately it's not something looked upon as valuable or even necessary by many. While I had thought my credentials coupled with my enthusiasm would lead to a position, I had to face the reality that it was not going to happen. For the most part, I could blame it all on poor timing. With the economy being so volatile, funeral homes are always setting priorities and looking at resources that are cost-effective. And with technology being so widely used, online resources including websites, suggested readings, interactive videos, and daily e-mail affirmations are what are offered the bereaved by most funeral homes. It's unfortunate because not everyone is computer savvy and/or has access to a computer, so anything offered on a funeral home website may go unnoticed. And even people with computer access do not want to sit and read about how they may or may not feel. At a time of loss, outreach and personal contact are so important!

Consequently, a second career in Funeral Home Aftercare was not to be and my bereavement work has been informal, intermittent and without compensation. But that's okay, because I believe I am doing what I am supposed to be doing.

First, I am letting grieving individuals know I understand.

> To be truly helpful, the people in your support system must appreciate the impact this death has had on you. They must understand that in order to heal, you must be allowed—even encouraged—to mourn long after the death. And they must encourage you to see mourning not as an enemy to be vanquished but as a necessity to be experienced as a result of having loved. (Wolfelt, *The Journey* 119)

And secondly and most importantly, I let them know that there are no timetables when it comes to grief. As Ann Hood so eloquently explains from her own experience:

> Grief is not linear. People kept telling me that once this happened or that passed, everything would be better. Some people gave me one year to grieve. They saw grief as a straight line, with a beginning, middle, and end. But it is not linear. It is disjointed. One day you are acting like a normal person. You may even

manage to take a shower. Your clothes match. You think the autumn leaves look pretty, or enjoy the sound of snow crunching under your feet.

Then a song, a glimpse of something, or maybe even nothing sends you back into the hole of grief. It is not one step forward, two steps back. It is a jumble. It is hours that are all right, and weeks that aren't. Or it is good days and bad days. Or it is the weight of sadness making you look different to others and nothing helps. (*Comfort* 52-53)

And lastly, I am educating others to realize that loss comes in many forms and is not limited to a specific age group.

Any loss is upsetting. It isn't just a death that upsets your sense of balance. It is important to remember that divorce, moving, financial loss, children leaving home and illness are among the many other experiences that can also have devastating effects on you.

These kinds of experiences happen to everyone. They knock you off balance. You must recover that balance before life can go on. (Deits 36-37)

In helping others no matter what form, whether through my bereavement work or through my volunteering at a local children's hospital and a Ronald McDonald House, I have found that I am helping myself. It helps me not only keep things in perspective but also to rise above any sadness over losing Al.

As You Help Others

You will find that
you are important,
you are wanted,
you are needed.
Because you, yourself, have
experienced grief, you are better able to understand
the heartaches of others.
As you lift a hand to help another,
you are lifting
yourself.
(Grollman, *Living* 104)

After I retired from the field of education, I initially filled my days with volunteer work and travel until I assumed a very unexpected but joyful role as a grandparent. My first grandchild Kendra was born September 9, 2011. And because I was no longer teaching, I was able to help out with my granddaughter once my daughter and my son-in-law returned to their jobs after each took consecutive parental leaves.

I'll be truthful when I say that initially the thought of taking care of an infant four out of five days a week seemed daunting! But as Kendra got older and my days with her became fewer, I felt saddened but so thankful for the time I had been able to spend with her. Even today I often reminisce about the numerous activities that filled our days, including stroller walks, visits to the playground, and story hours at the library.

Within a year of my granddaughter's birth I was blessed with the birth of my son's first child Patrick. I cried when I saw that his middle name was listed as Joseph, Al's legal first name. And then several years later Patrick became a big brother to Nicholas.

The births of my grandchildren had a tinge of sadness because I realized how much Al would be missing and also how much they would be missing not having Al present in their lives. But I was determined that they would grow up knowing him.

When I became Nona with Kendra's birth, my daughter and I chose the name Poppy for my husband. And so it is still today that my grandchildren are growing up seeing pictures of Poppy and hearing stories about him!

My friend in France once told me that the French have a saying, "Les petits enfants sont le dessert de la vie!" Translated it means, "Grandchildren are the dessert of life." And I always like to add, "and calorie free!" What a treat!

Throughout the Years

It has been more than two decades since Al died, and I still have my occasional moments of disbelief that so much time has passed. I think it's the realization also that I am that much older! It's definitely a rude awakening as some might call it.

I know at times some people felt that I hadn't moved on because I never went out with anyone for seventeen years. But during those years I did things I thought I never would do—alone. I traveled both domestically and internationally. And I set a mental timetable for downsizing, sold my house and moved to a condo. But even with all this, I knew I would never completely get over losing my husband. And I was always encouraged by Ashenburg's statement that "'recovery' should be understood as in quotation marks, because in many ways a serious loss never stops being a loss. But even the most searing bereavement can eventually be integrated into an ongoing life" (151).

In the introduction to her book, *In Lieu of Flowers, A Conversation for the Living*, Nancy Cobb likewise explains this idea of integration and ties it in with the mistaken notion of the so-called closure that people seek after a death.

> Grief is ongoing and individual. It can take weeks and months and years to fathom on a personal level, and even on a national level....
>
> When a person dies, a relationship does not end—it changes and continues, just as the living do. The bond, like the grief, is ongoing, ebbing and flowing with the passage of time, but enlivened in every cherished memory and in every story told....So when we use closure, I think what we really mean is connection. Closure suggests completion. Rather than closure, we long for continuity, for one last chance to tell the person how much he or she was loved and will be missed....We are desperate to keep that bond alive. Our grief is a natural opening where a link between the living and the dead is forged, and once we are able to incorporate it into our hearts and souls, we understand that grief is an integral part of life....Grieving is as natural as breathing, for if we have lived and loved, surely we will grieve. We must grieve, in our own separate ways, for as long as it takes, until that grief becomes a part of us, a grief that will end only with our own deaths, when the eternal cycle of mourning begins again. (viii-ix)

So when unexpected emotions used to render me motionless, I would not be hard on myself or wonder what was going on. I would remember that "survivors need to be patient with themselves" (Hersh 23). And I would think of the following words and allow myself the time to be still and quiet:

> Loss of any kind throws us back on ourselves—into that psychic space where the self can break down before it begins to heal. Healing has its own rhythm and tempo—long pauses of inertia, when it feels like nothing is happening or ever will again....we are often obliged to abide in the inertial state of "no thing" before change can happen of its own accord. (Falk 150-151)

As unexpected news would crop up over the years, my first impulse would always be to call Al at work and to share the update with him. But the sadness of his death used to stab me each time. But I knew that was okay. As Kübler-Ross and Kessler affirm:

> The reality is that you will grieve forever. You will not "get over" the loss of a loved one; you will learn to live with it. You will heal, and you will rebuild yourself around the loss you have suffered. You will be whole again, but you will never be the same. Nor should you be the same, nor would you want to. (230)

There used to be days when I'd be smiling and feeling upbeat even when there might be clouds outside. And on other days even with the sun shining, sadness and fear crept in. But just like that helpless tree that survived the winter, I somehow knew I would survive! "Often during the cold winter she had questioned the reason, but even while she had trembled with anxiety she had felt an inner voice—a small but steady voice—which remained fluid and alive when everything else in her had seemed paralyzed (Fahy, *The Tree* 9)."

I know I've changed so much during the time since Al died. In a sense I was forced to change in order to move forward and survive. But once I did, I realized I liked the person I had become.

However, that growth didn't push Al out. Instead his spirit filled the hole in my heart that his death left. And as a result, I believe he's with me always!

> Those whom we have loved and loved us in return will always live on in our hearts and minds. As you continue on your journey, know that you are richer and stronger, and that you know yourself better now. You have transformed and evolved.
> You have loved, lost and survived.
> You can find gratitude for the time you and your loved one shared together, as short as that seems to have been. Time helps as you continue healing and live on.
> Yours is the grace of life, death, and love.
> (Kübler-Ross and Kessler 225-226)

Spring Came Along Totally Unexpected

Although people had told me so many times that I should be dating, that I shouldn't be growing older alone, I really had no interest. In hindsight I sometimes wonder if it was really disinterest or fear that kept me from meeting anyone. Some colleagues even offered to set up an account on a dating site for me. But I wanted no part of it.

And so it came as quite a surprise when I received a Christmas card along with a letter from the father of a former student. At that time he was a guidance counselor at a career tech school and one of his counselees was the daughter of a friend/former colleague of mine. In his letter he explained that she had recently mentioned me on more than one occasion. In fact, she must have had matchmaking in mind because she also informed him that I was a widow. Somehow he didn't know that his wife had in fact sent me a sympathy card, years before when Al died.

He also must not have remembered that I had gone to his daughter's service when she died as an adult because he mentioned her death as well in his letter. Julie Joy had been chronically ill a good part of her life and I had tried to stay in touch with her after she graduated from high school. And maybe because of that he commented that he always remembered my kindness towards her.

What I didn't know was that his wife had died a few years before and that she had become ill a few years after his daughter had died. That explained no longer receiving a Christmas card from his wife and him. And actually, it was because I had been on his wife's card list that he found my contact info in her address book.

Three-quarters into his letter he got to the point. He wasn't sure if I went out much and wondered if I might be interested in meeting up for coffee. He told me he wouldn't be pesky if I didn't respond, but he did give his phone number if I was interested.

While I later found out that his intention was not to rile me with wondering if I got out much, it did. In my mind I wondered if he was looking for a needy widow. And that I was not!

I decided to send him a photo Christmas card of my grandchildren and me along with a note. I let him know that my husband had died back in 1999. I also let him know that I had been away in Sicily when his wife died. Hence my not knowing that fact. Then for some unknown reason which later surprised me, I told him I would call him at the end of the week.

While I later regretted that "promise," I knew I had to

call him. But I texted him first to see if it was a good time to call. He was chaperoning a school dance but was able to talk a little. He kept clearing his throat so I wasn't sure if he was nervous or it was just a habit. He didn't bring up going out for coffee and neither did I. To be truthful I can't remember what we talked about.

But the following week he used my tactic and texted me one afternoon to see if it was a good time for a phone call. I told him I was cleaning for the holidays but could use a break. He called and we talked. Somehow, someway, by the time the conversation ended, it wasn't coffee that was on the agenda but dinner at his nephew's restaurant the day after Christmas. I hung up in panic mode and wasn't sure what had just happened. In his letter he had mentioned meeting for coffee to see if we had anything in common, and now we would be going out for dinner after two short phone calls.

I had so much on my mind with Christmas coming up in a few days. And now this? I knew I wouldn't be able to put it out of my mind. So the next day I texted my daughter and asked her to call me when she had a chance.

Since texting had become our most convenient mode of communication, I answered the phone and immediately assured Jenny that I wasn't sick. But then I began to cry as I told her that someone had asked me out and that it was supposed to have been for coffee and somehow ended up as a meal. Without missing a beat my daughter asked, "Does this mean I'm going to have a new daddy?" I knew the question was her way of trying to put me at ease; instead it raised my angst. She told me that coffee would be awkward, that we were too old to go out just for a drink, and that dinner was perfect. I wasn't convinced but at least I had told someone.

James initially used the avoidance technique in dealing with this whole new situation in my life. Actually it was difficult for me as well. I waited about a month before I even let my friends know I was "seeing" someone. I just couldn't say the word "dating."

I should note that I almost stood up Richard for that dinner. But I did show up and we were at the restaurant three hours! And that was just the beginning for us!

Fast-forward almost six years later; Richard and I are a LAT couple—living apart together! Neither of us is interested in getting married or living together. We have found we need our own space, but love being together and doing things together.

I think we mirror what Zenith Gross described as the relationship she and (her) Richard had years after each of their spouses had died. "We try to share as much of each other's lives and families as we can, and believe that our commitment to each other is no longer about family-and-home building as when we were young, but rather to help each other age as gracefully and with as much joy, health, and dignity as possible" (7).

And because both Richard and I have lost a spouse, we understand that our relationship is different from the ones we had before. We have no one to be jealous of and we both speak freely about our deceased spouses and the lives we shared with them.

Both James and Jenny realize that Richard will never replace their father; he's just a nice addition. And he's Big

Guy to my three grandchildren. As Patrick, who gave him that name because of his tall stature, once explained, "He's big and he's a guy!"

Richard and I sometimes talk about the table for four waiting for us after we die. Al and Carol are holding our places when we shall all be reunited once again.

Never would I have imagined myself with another man. I wasn't looking for one and I wasn't expecting one to come into my life seventeen years after Al's death. But things happen for a reason. And I must admit that I'm happy I have someone at this point in my life. Plus I'm fairly sure Al is looking down with a smile on his face!

And the Grief Goes On

Years ago Judith Viorst, a well-known author, wrote a book entitled *Necessary Losses*. The subtitle explains the book as *The Loves, Illusions, Dependencies, and Impossible Expectations That All of Us Have To Give Up in Order To Grow*. However, her introduction breaks it down more simply.

> When we think of loss we think of the loss, through death, of people we love. But loss is a far more encompassing theme in our life. For we lose not only through death, but also by leaving and being left, by changing and letting go and moving on. And our losses include not only our separations and departures from those we love, but our conscious and unconscious losses of romantic dreams, impossible expectations, illusions of freedom and power, illusions of safety—and the loss of our own younger self, the self that thought it would always be unwrinkled and invulnerable and immortal. (15-16)

I remember when my father died in 1987 at the age of sixty-eight, my own mortality smacked me in the face. I had lost grandparents, aunts, and uncles, even a cousin; but his death had a profound effect on me. My reasoning was that if this man who with my mom had brought me into this world could die, then I, his offspring, was susceptible to this end as well.

I don't think I was affected in the same way when Al died and later when my mother died. What really brought me face to face with my own mortality once again was a minor heart attack that came on totally unexpected in October 2021. I had been following an exercise routine that included yoga, Pilates, walking and some weight training; all my levels were decent, plus I had been watching my diet. So trying to accept this medical issue was and still is difficult today even though I have traced it to genetics.

I feel like it's aged me. Somehow my pride over my good health can no longer be! Now my health is considered compromised because of the two stents the cardiologist inserted in my arteries and I have to take additional meds to prevent another attack from happening.

"We will mourn the loss of others. But we are also going to mourn the loss of our selves—of earlier definitions that our images of self depend upon. For the changes in our body redefine us" (Viorst 265).

When people ask how I'm doing, I usually respond that I'm doing okay but that my head still isn't straight. How do I explain that? A non-death loss has hit me and I haven't yet fully accepted it!

In the beginning I cried a lot. Not as much now. But I'm not the self I was BHA (Before Heart Attack). And I'm still grieving the loss of that self!

I often think about the fact that I am alive and capable of doing so much, unlike many others who have been hit with a debilitating disease or fatal illness. I know I have no right to complain. But I also know from my journey through grief over losing my Al that I am experiencing another loss that must be acknowledged and dealt with in my own time.

My mom used to say, "Life can be difficult. That's why it's for the living!" I think her words told to me so many years ago have a message for me today. Life is not easy; life is not fair. But as I get up each day, I should be thankful for the day and hopeful that I can meet any obstacles big or small that might come my way.

What About God?

DURING THE YEARS IMMEDIATELY FOLLOWING Al's death to the present my relationship with God has gone through several changes. Initially, I think I was questioning my belief in His presence in my life. I did continue attending services at the parish where we had belonged prior to Al's death and where his funeral had taken place. But that didn't last too long.

The problem lay not only in my anger towards God for having "taken" my husband from me; part of my struggle went back to the year before Al died. He had been involved with a parish organization; in fact, he had been one of the officers. But he distanced himself from both the group and the church after the members got into a fist-fighting debate over deciding how to use funds for a Right to Life project. I can still remember the evening of that heated dispute. Al came home sad and very upset. He believed the entire situation was ironic and hypocritical. Grown men were ready to harm each other over a project concerning the sacredness of life.

But I think what hurt Al the most was that no one cared later that he was no longer part of both the organization and the parish as a whole. And yet when he died, members came to the wake and "paid their respects." Some may have even attended the funeral Mass. However, all I could think was that it was a little too late!

Sometimes I wonder why I didn't have his funeral at the church where he had been baptized and belonged a good part of his life. My children had even suggested it. But for some reason I chose the place where Al's faith had been challenged. Was I trying to prove something? Was I trying to show that I could "turn the cheek"? I still question myself even to this day.

And then several months after Al's death, I found my anger towards God and that parish worsened. So I totally stopped going to church. It seemed like the logical decision. And I felt no guilt over this self-imposed schism.

Nevertheless, that split did not last long. And it was not remorse but rather an inner longing that made me search for a new place sometime during that first year; I missed organized religion! But I soon found out that not even a new church could enable me to make amends with God and make me believe in Him as I had before. "Religion is not an insurance policy offering protection against the cruel blows of sudden death. Religion does not preclude grief nor inoculate you against suffering. Doubts are part of the cycle of faith" (Grollman, *Spiritual* 185).

At some point I confessed to a priest that I was angry at God and that I no longer believed in Him. His response has stayed with me so many years later. He told me that the very fact that I was angry at God showed that I did believe in Him. And then he told me it was perfectly okay to be angry with God. After all, even the Bible tells us of people like Job who felt anger towards Him as well. Maybe Rabbi Grollman was right when he said, "It's okay then to be angry at God. God can take it" (*Spiritual* 186).

But what about the ensuing years? After some time I became disillusioned with my "new" church that had acted as a refuge for me in spite of my disbelief. This disenchantment came as a result of the inadequate response to my request for a support group for widows and widowers. However, that one omission seemed to have much more of an effect on me. It made me realize that I no longer wanted to be committed to or associated with one particular place of worship.

So for many years I "church-hopped." I would attend services wherever I wanted and/or the opportunity presented itself. And yes, there were times when I did not attend Mass; and I felt no guilt like that impressed upon me by my religion and by my parents when I was a child growing up.

Although I remained a Catholic, I came to believe that spirituality more so than religion is important in a person's life. About a year before she died, a dear former colleague offered me two sayings that give truth to this distinction. She never told me their sources so in my heart and mind I attribute them to her. Sylvia never questioned my beliefs, but I think she somehow sensed my struggle with my faith and organized religion. "Go out and spread the Good News and sometimes use words." And in connection to that, "You may be the only Gospel your brothers and sisters read."

I'm not exactly sure at what point I began attending Mass more regularly at a church where my heart brother David belonged. I still church-hopped on occasion, but found myself more times than not at that same church. However, my unpleasant past experiences kept me from committing myself. Organized religion, which I had embraced so totally at one time, no longer seemed to have a strong hold on me. Maybe deep down inside I equated organized religion with belief in God. And so many years after Al's death I was still continuing to question my belief in Him and my closeness to Him.

Maybe Al's experience with the Church that year before he died is all part of the journey I have been on to resolve my relationship with God. I'm convinced it's not what I believe as much as how I live my life.

I think my son James said it so well with what he wrote on the back of the leaflets distributed at Al's funeral: "My father has cast his light on everyone here today. Please remember him for his kindness and goodwill to everyone he encountered, his commitment to his work, his friends and family, and incorporate his light into your life."

So where am I with God today?

About six years ago I followed my heart brother to still another church, the difference being that I no longer church-hopped, and attended Mass there on a regular basis. I saw it as a safe haven for people of all backgrounds, life situations, etc., but I still wouldn't commit/join. I think the past still haunted me and I always feared being hurt or disappointed again.

Right now I seem to be at a crossroads, not sure of staying or leaving. But I don't think I will do the church-hopping again. I have come to realize that no one parish is perfect because the leaders are not perfect. They are human and subject to human error and behavior like the rest of us.

I continue to question my faith, especially when bad things continue to happen to good people. Maybe I'm still holding on to that all loving and all powerful image of God that was instilled in me as a child and confuses me as an adult. And perhaps I'm placing the burden on God more than on man's free will. I'm just not sure at times.

However, I am hoping that when I die, people will remember me like Al for my kindness and goodwill. AMEN!

Afterword

WHEN I WROTE THE ORIGINAL MANUSCRIPT FOR my scholarly project, I entitled it *Neverending Winter: A Journey of Grief*. However, in the course of working on the expanded version I decided to change the subtitle to *A Journey Through Grief*. At that time I believed modifying just one word was so important and was symbolic of where I had been and where I was going. As Kristen Carlson discovered after her husband's sudden death, "...I realized I needed to let Grief in. I needed to surrender. Grief would lead me and I would move through it, no matter what it brought. There was no escape route as an option" (27).

But going through grief does not necessarily mean giving it up and/or being totally free from it.

> You as a griever, have a right, whatever the loss, not only to grieve your loss, but to keep your grief. You do not "get over" grief. Anyone who says that you can, or tells you they did, is not to be believed. Grief keepers accept their grief and weave it into the fabric

of their lives.... As pilgrims on a long journey to a far place, be proud to be a grief keeper. (Smith 9, 231)

After Richard came into my life I realized that a new relationship would not mean forgetting about losing Al so many years before. I knew he would continue to be a part of me and that I would always hold on to my grief in one form or another.

From the first days of our relationship Richard helped me to understand that I was entering a new phase of my life. Like perennial flowers that bloom again after lying dormant during the winter, I would begin to look at life differently. While I would not forget the long winter I had endured following my husband's death, I would begin to enjoy the season of spring that had entered my life.

As a result I have once again made a change to the title of my book which I believe best encapsulates the past twenty plus years of my life—*After Winter Comes Spring: A Journey Through Grief and Beyond.* After reading my book I hope you will agree that the new title more aptly describes it. And please notice I have purposely used the present tense "comes" rather than the past "came" to give hope to those of you who have lost a loved one. The dreariness of grief sometimes stays for years but spring does come along at some point, suggesting new growth not only in nature but within ourselves, thus giving us a sense of renewed life and a fresh start!

BE WELL ALWAYS!

Works Cited

Ashenburg, Katherine. *The Mourner's Dance*. New York: North Point Press, 2002.

Attig, Thomas. *The Heart of Grief*. New York: Oxford University Press, Inc., 2000.

Becker, Ernest. *The Denial of Death*. New York: Simon & Schuster, 1973.

Bouvard, Marguerite (in collaboration with Evelyn Gladu). *The Path Through Grief*. Dallas, Texas: Taylor Publishing Co., 1988.

Brenner, Anne. *Mourning and Mitzvah*. Vermont: Jewish Lights Publishing, 1993.

Brothers, Dr. Joyce. *Widowed*. New York: Simon and Schuster, 1990.

Carlson, Kristine. *Heartbroken Open—A Memoir Through Loss and Self Discovery*. New York: Harper Collins Publishers, 2010.

Cobb, Nancy. *In Lieu of Flowers*. New York: Pantheon Books, 2001.

Cook, Alicia Skinner and Daniel Dworkin. *Helping the Bereaved*. New York: Basic Books, 1992.

Corr, Charles A., Clyde M. Nabe and Donna M. Corr. *Death &Dying, Life & Living* 5th edition. Belmont, CA: Thomson Wadsworth, 2006.

Crenshaw, David B. *Bereavement*. New York: Continium Publishing Co., 1990. "Life Span Issues and Assessment and Intervention" *Handbook of Thanatology*. David Balk, ed. Northbrook, Illinois: ADEC, 2007, pp 227-234.

Deits, Bob. *Life After Loss- A Personal Guide Dealing with Death, Divorce, Job Change, Relocation*. Tucson: Fisher Books, 1992.

DeSpelder, Lynne Ann and Albert Lee Strictland. *The Last Dance Seventh Edition*. New York: McGraw-Hill, 2005.

De Saint Exupery, Antoine. *Wind, Sand and Stars*. New York: Reynal & Hitchcock, 1939.

Diamant, Anita. *Saying Kaddish*. New York: Shocken Books, 1998.

Didion, Joan. *Blue Nights*. New York: Vintage Books, 2012. *The Year of Magical Thinking*. New York: Alfred A. Knopf, 2005.

Doka, Kenneth J. "Disenfranchised Grief" *Disenfranchised Grief*. Kenneth J. Doka, ed. New York: Lexington Books, 1989, pp. 3-11.

Du Marier, Daphne. "Death and Widowhood." *In the Midst of Winter: Selections from the Literature of Mourning*. Mary Jane Moffat, ed. New York: Random House, 1982, pp. 147-155.

Fahy, Mary. *The Tree That Survived the Winter*. New Jersey: Paulist Press, 1989. *A Time for Leaving*. New Jersey: Paulist Press, 2007.

Falk, Florence. *On My Own—The Art of Being a Woman Alone*. New York: Harmony Books, 2007.

Gibran, Kahlil. *The Prophet*. New York: Alfred A. Knopf, 1923.

Ginsburg, Genevieve Davis. *Widow to Widow*. Tuscon, Arizona: Fisher Books, 1995.

Goudge, Eileen. *Woman in Red*. New York: Vanguard Press, 2007.

Greene, Phyllis. *It Must Have Been Moonglow- Reflections on the First Years of Widowhood*. New York: Villard Books, 2001. "Re: A Fellow Widow." Message to the Author. 14 Sept. 2002. Email.

Grollman, Earl A. *Living When A Loved One Has Died*. 3rd Edition. Boston: Beacon Press, 1995. "Spiritual Support after Sudden Loss." *Living with Grief after Sudden Loss*. Kenneth J. Doka, ed. Washington, DC: Hospice Foundation of America, 1996, pp.185-186.

Gross, Zenith Henkin. *Seasons of the Heart*. California: New World Library, 2000.

Guggenheim, William and Judy Guggenheim. *Hello from Heaven*. New York: Bantam Books, 1995.

Hersh, Stephen, P. "After Heart Attack and Stroke." *Living with Grief after a Sudden Loss*. Kenneth J. Doka, ed. Washington, DC: Hospice Foundation of America, 1996, pp. 17-24.

Hood, Ann. *Comfort*. New York: W. W. Norton & Co., 2008. *The Knitting Circle*. New York: W.W. Norton & Co., 2007.

Hughes, Marylou. *Bereavement and Support: Healing in

a Group Environment. Washington, DC : Taylor and Francis, 1995.

Jackson, Edgar N. *The Many Faces of Grief*. Nashville: The Partheon Press, 1977.

Johnson, Catherine and O. Duane Weeks. "How to Develop A Successful Aftercare Program" Duane O. Weeks and Catherine Johnson, ed. *When All the Friends Have Gone*. New York: Baywood Publishing Company, Inc. 2001, pp. 5-23.

Just, Ward. *The Weather in Berlin*. New York: Houghton Mifflin Co., 2002.

Kauffman, Jeffrey. "Intraphysic Dimensions of Disenfranchised Grief." *Disenfranchised Grief*. Kenneth J. Doka, ed. New York: Lexington Books, 1989, pp. 25-29.

Kübler-Ross, Elisabeth and David Kessler. *On Grief and Grieving*. New York: Scribner, 2005.

Lambin, Helen Reichert. *The Death of a Hisband- Reflections for a Grieving Wife*. Chicago: ACTA Publications, 1998.

Lewis, C.S. *A Grief Observed*. New York: Bantam Books, 1976.

Lieberman, Morton. *Doors Close, Doors Open*. New York: G.P. Putnam's Sons, 1996.

Lindemann, Eric. "Symptomatology and Management of Acute Grief." *Death—Current Perspectives*. 4th edition. John B. Williamson and Edwin S. Sneidman. Mountain View, CA: Mayfield Publishing Co., 1995. 185-195.

Maguire, Gregory. *Wicked—The Life and Times of the Wicked Witch of the West*. New York: Harper Collins Publishers, 1995.

Manning, Doug. *Don't Take My Grief Away from Me.* Oklahoma City: Insight Books, Inc. 1979/2005.

Miletech, Lyn. "Defining the Essence of Aftercare." *When All the Friends Have Gone.* Duane O. Weeks and Catherine Johnson, ed. New York: Baywood Publishing Company, Inc. 2001, pp. 25-34.

Moss, MS and S. Moss. "Remarriage of Widowed Persons, A Triadic Relationship." *Continuing Bonds.* Dennis Klass, Phyllis R. Silverman and Steven L. Nickman, ed. Philadelphia: Taylor & Francis, 1996.

Neimeyer, Robert A. *Lessons of Loss.* Florida: PsychoEducational Resources, Inc., 2000.

Noppe, Lloyd D. "Catching Your Breath with Dr. Attig" *The Forum.* Volume 33, Issue 3 July 2007. p.5

Nuland, Sherwin B. *How We Die.* New York: Alfred A. Knopf, 1993.

Peabody, Kathleen L. and Margaret L. Mooney. *Widows Are Special, They Know They Will Rise Again.* Carlsbad: Sharp Publishing, 1994.

Picoult, Jodi. *Nineteen Minutes.* New York: Atria Books, 2007.

Prigerson, Holly G. and Selby C. Jacobs. "All the Doctors Just Suddenly Go." *Journal of American Medical Association.* Sep 19, 2001; 286 (11):1369-76. http://jama.ama-assn.org/cgi/content/abstract/286/11/1369.

Rando, Terese. *How To Go On Living When Someone You Love Dies.* New York: Bantam Books, 1991. "Unresolved Grief." *Death—Current Perspectives.* 4th edition. John B. Williamson and Edwin S. Sneidman. Mountain View, CA: Mayfield Publishing Co.,1995,p. 203.

Rapoport, Nessa. *A Woman's Book of Grieving*. New York: William Morrow & Co., Inc. 1994.

Sanders, Catherine M. *Surviving Grief...and Learning to Live Again*. New York: John Wiley & Sons, Inc., 1992.

Schraff, Laura and Alex Tresniowski. *An Invisible Thread*. New York: Howard Books, 2011.

Smith, Harold Ivan. *Grief Keeping Learning How Long Grief Lasts*. New York: The Crossroad Publishing Co., 2004.

Strout, Elizabeth. *Olive Kitteridge*. New York: Random House, Inc., 2008.

The New American Bible. New York: Thomas Nelson, Publishers, 1976.

Viorst, Judith. *Necessary Losses*. New York: Simon & Schster, 1986.

Weeks, Duane O. "Ritualistic Downsizing and the Need for Aftercare." Duane O. Weeks and Catherine Johnson,ed. *When All the Friends Have Gone*. New York: Baywood Publishing Company, Inc. 2001, pp.188-197.

Wolfelt, Alan D. *How To Reach Out for Help When You Are Grieving*. Batesville Management Services, 1993. *The Journey Through Grief- Reflections on Healing*. Fort Collins, Colorado: Companion Press, 1997. *The Understanding Your Grief Support Group Guide*. Fort Collins, Colorado: Companion Press, 2004.

Zeitlin, Steve and Ilana Harlow. *Giving a Voice to Sorrow*. New York: The Berkley Publishing Group, 2001.

Zucker, Arthur. "Ethical and Legal Issues and End-of-Life Decision Making." *Handbook of Thantology*. David Balk, ed. Northbrook, Illinois: ADEC, 2007, pp.103-112.

Acknowledgments

I HESITATE IN NAMING NAMES HERE FOR FEAR I'LL forget someone and regret it for years to come. However, I will mention several.

First, grazie to my grandmother Giovanna (aka Nana Jennie) and my mother Antonina (aka Anna). In 2015 I traveled to my grandparents' birthplace in Sicily and while there I pondered the fact that my grandmother, my mother, and I had all become widows at different points of our lives but in the course of a single century. While we all dealt with the loss of our spouses in different ways, I do believe that my nana and my mom influenced my journey as a widow because of their strength and their faith.

Thanks to my dad! He always called me Milly when I was growing up and I never knew why nor did I question it. In looking at the meaning of this name I wonder if he knew something then that I couldn't have known.

I am forever grateful to Al for telling me years ago to live my life to the fullest. And to Richard for making sure

I continue to do that, and for keeping me sane during the final writing process.

Love and hugs to my children and grandchildren. They have been part of this journey which hasn't always been easy. But having them with me has made all the difference.

Tremendous thanks to Steven and Dawn Porter of Stillwater River Publications for helping me bring to fruition that which has been in the making for so many years.

And lastly, my deepest gratitude to anyone who has been part of this phase of my life since 1999, personally, professionally, or otherwise. You know who you are! And while your names are not listed here, they are forever embedded in my heart!

About the Author

ANN BOULET WAS BORN AND grew up in Providence, Rhode Island. She lived there until moving to Smithfield in 1988 and still resides there today.

Ann was an educator for many years. During her career she taught English and French to junior high and high school students, Journalism to high school juniors and seniors, English and Communications in a veterans' program at a local college, and English as a Second Language to adults in an evening school program.

Her interest in the field of bereavement began several years after her husband Al died suddenly of a massive heart attack New Year's Eve afternoon just before Y2K. She earned a Certificate in Thanatology from Mount Ida College in Newton, Massachusetts and became Certified in Thanatology (CT) through the Association for Death

Education and Counseling. She has given presentations on death and dying to various groups and does informal bereavement outreach.

Ann loves a good novel but does read other genres of literature. She advocates bibliotherapy for anyone dealing with grief.

She tries to stay healthy by exercising, walking, practicing yoga, and doing Pilates.

In her retirement Ann loves helping out with her grandchildren and volunteering at the Ronald McDonald House of Providence and the Ronald McDonald Family Room at Hasbro Children's Hospital. She also enjoys traveling here and abroad. Her most memorable trip was to Spain in 2019 when she walked the Camino de Santiago and received the Compostela certificate upon completion.

Made in the USA
Middletown, DE
17 January 2023